Literacy Leadership Teams

Collaborative Leadership for Improving and Sustaining Student Achievement

Pamela S. Craig, Ph.D.

Routledge
Taylor & Francis Group
New York London

First published 2010 by Eye On Education

Published 2013 by Routledge
711 Third Avenue, New York, NY 10017, USA
2 Park Square, Milton Park, Abingdon, Oxon OX14 4RN

Routledge is an imprint of the Taylor & Francis Group, an informa business

Library of Congress Cataloging-in-Publication Data

Craig, Pamela S.

Literacy leadership teams: collaborative leadership for improving and sustaining student achievement / by Pamela S. Craig, Ph.D.

p. cm.

ISBN 978-1-59667-125-6

1. Literacy. 2. Group work in education. 3. Educational leadership. 4. Academic achievement. I. Title.

LC149.C73 2009

428.0071—dc22

2009015894

ISBN: 978-1-596-67125-6 (pbk)

About the Author

Pamela S. Craig has taught high school English for 11 years. She earned her National Board Certification in Adolescent/Young Adult Language Arts in 1999 and recently recertified. Dr. Craig was named the 2001 English Teacher of the Year by the Florida Council of Teachers of English and currently serves as second vice president for the organization. She spent four years working with Florida Literacy and Reading Excellence through the University of Central Florida, helping schools throughout the state of Florida develop literacy plans to improve student achievement. She has presented nationally as well as locally on the topic of improving adolescent literacy. Most recently, Dr. Craig returned to the classroom to continue her research on practical ways to incorporate literacy within the English curriculum. She is passionate about the role of adolescent literacy in preparing students to become participating members of a democratic society and the role that teachers play to prepare students to achieve that goal.

Foreword

Seize the Data and Lead the Learning

If you could look back 100 years to the high school classroom of the past, you'd see some things easily recognizable, such as desks in rows and the teacher up front talking. What you wouldn't see are the countless ways we now have for teachers to use reading and writing in their content-area classrooms to engage students in learning. Today, secondary school teachers routinely use content literacy instructional approaches, such as read alouds or writing to learn, to ensure that students develop a sophisticated understanding of content. This is progress over previous decades in which these instructional routines were not yet known and were certainly not implemented.

But this progress is tempered by the fact that different teachers in different classrooms use different approaches to develop their students understanding (Fisher & Frey, 2007a). In fact, there is evidence that teachers work at odds with one another, with the result that students fail to develop the habits necessary for them be successful in the world of work or in college. For example, a teacher in first period might use *Cornell* notes whereas the teacher in second period uses outlining and the third period teacher doesn't care about notes at all. By no fault of their own, students who have these three teachers are unlikely to develop sophisticated note-taking skills that they can take with them to college.

Thankfully, progress is being made on this front. An increasing number of schools are developing schoolwide literacy initiatives that call for agreements on the skills and strategies students will know and be able to use when they graduate. Today we can mobilize the vast knowledgebase of content literacy in systematic and intentional ways to develop students' habits. But knowing that we *can* do it is different from knowing *how* to do it.

Having guessed or lucked my way through a number of school change projects over the years, I was thrilled to find *Literacy Leadership Teams: Collaborative Leadership for Improving and Sustaining Student Achievement.* Pamela Craig offers readers technical assistance in developing a literacy leadership team for secondary schools that can guide the school to increasingly higher levels of achievement. As she demonstrates, school literacy leadership teams can have a profound impact on the culture of the school. But more importantly, as Craig points out, the literacy leadership team can actually change what happens in the classroom. In other words, implementing a literacy leadership team can address the need for instructional consistency and focus. To accomplish this, Craig provides readers with

- background and research supporting the establishment of literacy leadership teams;
- specific leadership behaviors that are linked to improved student achievement; and
- guidelines and practices that develop and sustain successful literacy leadership teams.

The process Craig advocates is rational, well developed, and practical. From the formation of the team, to examining student achievement data, to developing, implementing, and evaluating the literacy plan, Craig provides insights and tools the reader can use. Suffice it to say that any school group that wants to improve student achievement will find nuggets worth their weight in gold in this book.

Douglas Fisher
San Diego State University

Acknowledgements

Rarely is the writing of a book accomplished by the writer alone. I could not have written this book had it not been for the support of my family who recognized the need for me to barricade myself in my study each Saturday morning as I etched out my ideas. I am especially grateful to my husband, Randy, for his patience and support throughout the process.

I am equally appreciative of the schools, teachers, reading coaches, and administrators who allowed me to work with them to help develop plans that specifically addressed their school's needs. The knowledge I gained while working with these committed individuals is contained within the pages of this book. We could not have accomplished our goals without the ongoing collaboration and support I received while working with Connie Kolosey, Lela-Ann Carroll, Sharon Feldhake, Donna Masi, Rose Napoli, Nancy Ragland, Pam Sudduth, Judy Terwilliger, and Jenieff Watson, all experts in their field and committed to improving literacy for all students.

This book would not have been possible without the knowledge and experience I gleaned while working with Florida Literacy and Reading Excellence (FLaRE). The days, months, and years we spent committed to supporting K-12 literacy in Florida benefited me professionally and personally in ways that will continue to influence me for years to come. For this experience I am grateful to Enrique Puig and all the FLaRE coordinators. I hold in my heart a special gratitude for my fellow cohorts who helped me and supported me through the writing of this book: Donna Garcia, Ruth Shaulis, Pam Rader, and Linda Tuschinski.

Finally, I am sincerely grateful to Dan Sickles who singled me out at an Association for Supervision and Curriculum Development conference and suggested I should write a book about my experiences. It is my sincere hope this book will benefit all who read it.

Free Downloads

Many of the tools discussed and displayed in this book are also available on the Routledge website as Adobe Acrobat files. Permission has been granted to purchasers of this book to download these tools and print them.

You can access these downloads by visiting www.routledge.com/9781596671256 and click on the Free Downloads tab.

Contents

1

Compelling *Whys*

Why Literacy?

Why Shared Leadership?

Why a Team?

Why One Plan?

One of the benefits of working in education is that we begin each year filled with anticipation as we welcome our new students into clean classrooms. Unfortunately, the newness wears off quickly, and we fall into our old routines, leading to a slow, steady letdown as the daily grind of schooling sets in. Despite our vision of future successes, we rarely change our way of work, which ultimately results in disappointment when the outcomes don't change. The added pressure from an increasingly critical public fueled by reports of low student achievement based on high-stakes testing feeds our own sense of helplessness. And so we end each year looking forward to the next, destined to repeat the process.

With 70% of all 8th grade students and 65% of all 12th grade students reading below grade level and with only 70% of students earning a high school diploma (Alliance for Excellent Education, 2008), it's easy to fall into the pit of despair rather than continue to seek options for improvement. Schools and teachers often feel bombarded with suggestions and initiatives for reform yet find it difficult to identify specific actions that will work within their own school culture. To add to our pressure, more often than not, reform initiatives are imposed upon schools rather than developed by schools. As a result, many teachers throw up their hands in despair and close their doors, effectively stalling any chance for real reform to occur.

This book shares practical ways to change the cycle from one of continuous disappointment to one based on continuous improvement by establishing collaborative, school-based literacy leadership teams (LLT). Three basic elements serve as the foundation for designing, implementing, and evaluating successful literacy plans: student achievement, research, and professional development. Each of these elements is linked to an outcome: improving student achievement, making informed decisions, and implementing professional development to change instructional practices, which, if incorporated effectively, will lead to improved student achievement. Throughout the cycle, the LLT evaluates each of these elements as it continues to make informed decisions to modify, sustain, and support the plan. In addition, I have link current research focusing on effective leadership characteristics to the specific actions suggested at each stage. Basically, my goal is to provide background and research supporting the establishment of literacy leadership teams, identify research-based leadership behaviors linked to improved student achievement, and provide specific guidelines and practices to develop and sustain a successful literacy leadership team plan.

> Questions to ponder

As you read through the text, you will note that I have included thought balloons to alert you to ideas and concepts addressed in each section. The purpose of thought balloons is to guide your questioning and to help you make links between practice, research, and application.

The book is organized into seven chapters: *Compelling Whys, Assembling the Team, Collecting and Analyzing Data, Developing the Plan, Implementing the Plan, Evaluating and Revising the Plan,* and *Sustaining the Team*. Each chapter provides specific examples of possible activities and actions to guide your team through the process of developing, implementing, supporting, and revising a working plan designed to meet the needs of your individual school.

Why Literacy?

> How will focusing on literacy improve student achievement?

Concerns about adolescent literacy are not new. Beginning in the early 1980s, *A Nation at Risk* (National Commission on Excellence in Education, 1983) warned of a crisis in adolescent literacy. More recently, *The Nation's Report Card: Reading 2007* (Lee, Grigg, & Donahue, 2007) lamented that although the lowest performing students are making gains in reading achievement, no significant gains have been made in overall reading proficiency for 8th grade students. Additionally, significant gaps exist between reading achievement of whites and minority students. Both reports suggest adolescents lack the literacy skills necessary to participate in an increasingly complex world. Unfortunately, while much emphasis has been placed on reading in grades K-3, relatively little has been placed on struggling adolescent readers (Biancarosa & Snow, 2004), fueling the resistance of secondary teachers to adopt literacy practices within content-area instruction. Yet as educators, we cannot ignore the glaring statistics reminding us that students who are not able to read proficiently are at risk for failure, not only within the school culture but within society as well.

Significant research supports the premise that a majority of struggling adolescent readers can read words but find it difficult to comprehend increasingly complex academic texts as they progress through school (Biancarosa & Snow, 2004). Adolescents can and do read on a regular basis. They just aren't reading academic texts at the level of proficiency required for achievement. However, they are quite comfortable reading for pleasure, or to acquire information that interests them, or that is linked to social considerations. Thus, determining how to modify instruction as a means of engaging students in academic reading becomes paramount to improving student achievement (Moje, Overby, Tysvaer, & Morris, 2008).

The complexity of literacy instruction moves beyond the basics (phonemic awareness, phonics, fluency, vocabulary, and comprehension) of teaching students how to read towards the goal of teaching students how to use reading as a tool for learning. This shift in thinking about the purpose of reading in secondary schools also reinforces the concept that all teachers, not just reading and language arts teachers, must address the issue of literacy within their own content areas. Secondary teachers not only require a deep understanding of the reading process, they must understand how to apply the process to their content reading.

To accomplish this lofty goal, teachers require intensive professional development and support to understand the theory and practice required to implement the instructional changes necessary for improving student achievement (Jacobs, 2008). Elizabeth Moje (2008) argues:

> If those interested in secondary school education were to reconceptualize learning in the subject areas as a matter of learning the different knowledge and ways of knowing, doing, believing, and communicating that are privileged to those areas, then perhaps a more compelling argument for integrating literacy teaching and subject area teaching could be made. It may even be the case that no argument would need to be made. (p. 99)

Helping teachers and administrators understand the connection between the act of reading and the act of learning as it differs between disciplines is necessary if we are to realize improved student achievement over time.

We begin with the premise that all students benefit from direct, explicit comprehension instruction along with effective instructional principles embedded in content-area classrooms (Biancarosa & Snow, 2004). Using this premise as a base, instructional focus must then shift from the more traditional content-knowledge curriculum to the more abstract content-literacy curriculum. In essence, we are asking teachers to focus not only on *what* students know but also to focus on *how* students know.

Think of this shift in these terms. For many years, secondary content-area teachers have focused on covering the content. Recognizing that many if not most of their students are unable to read the textbook provided, concerned teachers spend hours preparing copious notes, PowerPoints, and lectures to "give" students the knowledge they need to pass the exams. Teachers work hard at covering the content and become frustrated because students often forget the teaching from one year to the next. Now, teachers are being asked to consider teaching content-specific concepts rather than content-specific concrete details. Teachers are being asked to consider how students learn and process information rather than simply providing students with information. Teachers are being asked to teach their students to become literate consumers of their content rather than trivial pursuit experts of the content. The task is not an easy one. As Moje (2008) warns:

> The work and commitment required for developing an integrated approach to literacy teaching and learning in the secondary subject areas is enormous, requiring conceptual changes in our definitions, cultural changes in our practices, and structural changes in the enduring institutes of the secondary school and secondary teacher education. (p. 105)

For this shift in teaching to occur, teachers need time to work together within their content areas to design classroom instruction that motivates students to become engaged in self-directed learning. Teachers need time to share how changes in instruction are impacting student learning and, thus, student achievement. They must become experts within their discipline as well as experts in how students learn their discipline. However, it is not enough that teachers individually become experts at including content-literacy instruction within their own classrooms (Ivey & Fisher, 2006). These changes require teachers and administrators to work collaboratively and to engage in literacy professional development to more clearly define classroom instruction that leads to improved student achievement.

Why Shared Leadership?

Increasingly, administrators are being asked to become instructional leaders (Irvin, Metzler, & Dukes, 2007; Ivey & Fisher, 2006; Marzano, Waters, & McNulty, 2005). School-based leadership focused on improving student achievement is central to any successful reform initiative. Successful schools are led by principals who are members of the school community, who participate in the development and implementation of the plan, and who support the plan with resources.

Having said this, the reality is that principals are also expected to be the budget director, head disciplinarian, facilities manager, and community liaison. One principal once complained to me that he did not have the time nor the expertise to walk through classrooms on a regular basis and identify effective teaching. Another shared with me his frustration at the changes in principal expectations from when he first became a principal to now. Clearly, many principals are overwhelmed by the expectation that they become instructional leaders rather than business managers.

Leadership Characteristics Linked to Student Achievement

One way to address the issue of principal as instructional leader is to review literature and research focusing on leadership characteristics that are linked to improved student achievement. Marzano, Waters, and McNulty (2005) conducted a research meta-analysis focused on identifying leadership behaviors linked to student achievement. They examined 69 research studies completed or published between 1978 and 2001 involving 2,802 K-12 schools and specifically measured the effect size of leadership characteristics on student achievement, eventually identifying 21 leadership behaviors that positively impact student achievement.

The researchers recognize the improbability of individual principals possessing each of these characteristics and suggest these leadership behaviors can best be addressed by distributing these responsibilities through leadership teams that allow for other members of the school community to take leadership roles and to participate in designing, implementing, and sustaining effective changes (Marzano, Waters, & McNulty, 2005, pp. 41–61). As you read through this book, you will notice that I have highlighted the behaviors in bold print throughout as a way of reinforcing how these characteristics are implemented through the various suggested activities. Basically, incorporating the ideas and concepts suggested will provide for opportunities to implement 18 of the 21 leadership behaviors and responsibilities addressed in the research. These include:

- **Affirmation:** Effective leaders recognize and celebrate accomplishments while acknowledging failures through a fair, systematic process.
- **Change Agent:** Effective leaders are willing to challenge the status quo even if it entails temporarily creating disequilibrium within the school culture.
- **Contingent Rewards:** Effective leaders recognize and reward individual accomplishments based on individual performance versus longevity.
- **Communication:** Effective leaders develop strong lines of communication between teachers, students, and staff.
- **Culture:** Effective leaders create a school culture founded on a shared vision of the possibilities for what the school can become.
- **Flexibility:** Effective leaders adapt their behaviors and encourage individual expression of diverse opinions when the situation warrants.

- **Focus:** Effective leaders establish and maintain clear goals and provide clear direction towards achieving those goals.
- **Ideals and Beliefs:** Effective leaders possess well-defined beliefs about schools, teaching, and learning; share those beliefs with the staff; and demonstrate behaviors that are consistent with beliefs.
- **Input:** Effective leaders involve teachers in the design and implementation of important decisions and policies.
- **Intellectual Stimulation:** Effective leaders expose faculty and staff to current research, theories, and practices impacting effective schooling and provide time for systematic discussion.
- **Involvement in Curriculum, Instruction, and Assessment:** Effective leaders are involved in helping teachers design curriculum, assessments, and instruction.
- **Knowledge of Curriculum, Instruction, and Assessment:** Effective leaders possess extensive knowledge of effective instructional, curricular, and assessment practices and are able to provide conceptual guidance for teachers.
- **Monitoring/Evaluating:** Effective leaders monitor the effectiveness of school practices and their impact on student achievement.
- **Optimizer:** Effective leaders inspire teachers, serve as the driving force behind major initiatives, and maintain a positive attitude by expressing a belief in the staff to achieve its goals.
- **Order:** Effective leaders establish and reinforce clear routines, structures, and procedures to ensure order within the school community.
- **Resources:** Effective leaders allocate resources to ensure teachers have the necessary materials and equipment and to provide teachers with appropriate staff development needed to improve instruction.
- **Situational Awareness:** Effective leaders are aware of the details and undercurrents that may impact the school and are able to intercede when necessary.
- **Visibility:** Effective leaders are highly visible to students, teachers, and parents, making frequent classroom visits and contacts with students.

Although the plan does not directly address the remaining three leadership characteristics—discipline, outreach, and relationships—I am not suggesting that these characteristics are unimportant. Rather, all three are important to ensure successful plans, but these three are more specific for the principal and his personal relationships with the faculty, staff, and community.

Shared Leadership

Expecting one person to possess and/or to effectively integrate all 21 characteristics linked to improving student achievement seems unreasonable given the many responsibilities placed on principals. Considerable research exists suggesting that the traditional leadership model, which relies on the principal as the sole authority for making decisions and enforcing those decisions, rarely works (Copeland, 2003). Instead, the skilled principal leader is one who identifies other leaders within the school community and recruits them to build a solid leadership team. Some authors refer to this as "distributed leadership," a concept that suggests effective leadership is the result of the entire community working in sync to combine their knowledge and experiences for the common good (Spillane, Halverson, & Diamond, 2004). Leadership, then, is dependent on the collective body of the organization rather than limited to one specific individual. The end result is an ongoing, sustainable leadership which functions as "an organic activity, dependent on interrelationships and connections" (Hargreaves & Fink, 2003, p. 696).

Although the responsibility for improving student achievement may ultimately rest with the principal, effective principals understand they are more likely to achieve their goal when they work collaboratively with committed administrators and teacher leaders to achieve the desired goals and outcomes. Thus, principals interested in moving their schools towards improvement take the lead in developing shared leadership within the school community (Biancarosa & Snow, 2004; Copeland, 2003, Dufour & Eaker, 1998; Fisher & Frey, 2007; Irvin, Meltzer, & Dukes, 2007; Ivey & Fisher, 2006; Joyce & Showers, 2002; Marzano, Waters, & McNulty, 2005; Moeller & Pankake, 2006). Working together with a team of committed professionals within the school community will result in more positive outcomes and sustained changes.

Why a Team?

Research focused on schools that successfully overcome great odds link school-based leadership teams to continuous improvement. Successful literacy leadership teams can take on many of the leadership responsibilities outlined in research and help promote the type of school culture more clearly aligned with implementing successful changes. Well-developed literacy leadership teams serve as the driving force behind implementing and sustaining changes designed to impact classroom instruction and student achievement.

In addition to providing a vehicle for shared leadership, other reasons exist for establishing a team approach to addressing adolescent literacy. Leadership teams are designed to engage school staff in collaborative communities which serve as models for changing school culture. They allow all parties within a school to become participants in the change process which leads to whole-school support of initiatives. These teams focus on analyzing school data, researching possible solutions, assisting and supporting one another as they implement changes in instructional practices, and continuing to collect data to determine the effectiveness of the changes (Eaker, Dufour, & Dufour, 2002; Ivey & Fisher, 2006). Successful teams begin not with a plan in mind but rather with a goal of collectively developing a plan that best serves the school community.

Many books and articles have been written espousing the benefit of creating a collaborative culture within schools to implement successful reform. Dufour and Eaker (1998) argue "The most promising strategy for sustained, substantive school improvement is developing the ability of school personnel to function as professional learning communities" (p. xi). Ivey and Fisher (2006) stress the need to move beyond the existing culture of isolation that dominates many secondary schools towards a collaborative culture as a means of developing a school-wide commitment to improving student achievement. Lyons and Pinnell (2001) emphasize the need to establish a collaborative culture focused on supporting teacher learning, while Moeller and Pankake (2006) suggest that principals need to engage teachers in shared leadership. Several authors indicate successful schools work collaboratively to create a school vision for improved student achievement which then serves as a goal for all initiatives (DuFour & Eaker, 1998; Eaker, DuFour, & DuFour, 2002; Irvin, Meltzer, & Dukes, 2007). Finally, Marzano, Waters, & McNulty (2005) propose the development of school leadership teams based on the concept of "purposeful community" as essential for implementing successful school change. A purposeful community is one in which members work collaboratively "to accomplish goals that matter to all community members through agreed-upon processes" (p. 99).

All these authors share a belief in the necessity of creating a collaborative culture within each school community as the driving force behind establishing schoolwide goals for implementing effective changes linked to improved student achievement. The goal is to bring interested parties together to identify issues and concerns relating to student achievement and to establish a vehicle through which they can discuss and consider possible interventions. This differs from past initiatives traditionally imposed upon schools with little input from the school community.

Defining a Literacy Leadership Team

The literacy leadership team (LLT) becomes the vehicle combining the three essential elements impacting successful student achievement: literacy, leadership, and teams. The LLT serves as the guiding force behind the development and implementation of the Literacy Plan, which outlines specific initiatives designed to improve student achievement.

The team is made up of a cross-section of teacher leaders, administrators, and other members of the school community (which might include students and/or parents and other interested members of the greater community) committed to working in a collaborative group to identify areas of concern and to set goals for improving student achievement. The plan is determined through careful, ongoing analysis of teacher and student data collected through various means such as student assessment, student and teacher surveys, and observational data collected by administrators, teachers, and the team. The team engages in on-going professional dialogue and makes decisions based on review of current research, theories, and practices linked to improved student achievement as well as school-based data collection. The plan is fluid and able to be modified based on data (Figure 1.1, page 12). Its success is dependent upon schoolwide commitment to implementation combined with targeted, sustained professional development, administrative support, and continuing analysis.

Why One Plan?

As mentioned earlier, the key to success is implementing a schoolwide plan focusing on improving student literacy achievement. The success of the LLT and the resulting plan is dependent upon the emphasis placed on plan implementation. For serious, sustained change to take place, the literacy plan must take precedence over all other instructional and professional development plans. Other initiatives should be viewed as supplementary to ensuring success of the literacy plan, and their purpose clearly linked to the student achievement outcomes identified in the literacy plan. In other words, *all professional development provided to faculty must be linked to improving student achievement and, therefore, must be linked to the literacy plan.*

A mistake made by some schools is to relegate the plan to one of many being presented to the faculty, resulting in competition between plans and

Figure 1.1. Literacy Leadership Team

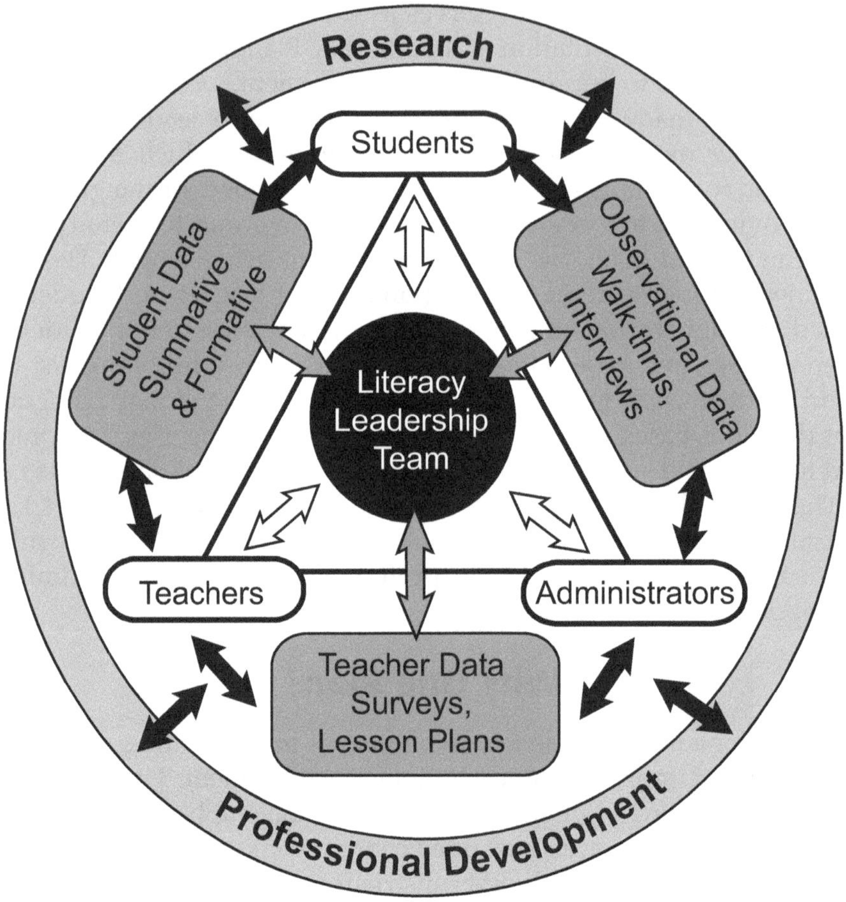

leading to frustration and a sense of overload by the faculty. For example, if part of the plan includes a technology component "as a tool for and a topic of literacy" (Biancarosa & Snow, 2006, p. 4), then the technology committee's professional development plan must emphasize the link between technology, literacy, and increasing student achievement. The professional development linked to technology must be provided in conjunction with the literacy plan rather than viewed as an alternative to the literacy plan's professional development. The emphasis should focus on how implementing the technology will directly correspond to improving student achievement.

Let me share a nonexample from one well-meaning but poorly implemented schoolwide initiative. The LLT was provided sustained time throughout the year to examine schoolwide data and develop schoolwide initiatives to begin the process of changing the literacy culture. The plan was developed in support with the principal and an administrator. The team left for the summer, confident its plan would be a success. Unfortunately, upon returning to school in the fall, several administrative changes resulted in derailing the literacy plan before it was even presented.

Over the summer, the administrator assigned to oversee schoolwide professional development (who was a different administrator than the one assigned to oversee the LLT) developed his own professional development plan without input from the LLT. Additionally, he called in a group of teachers who were not members of the LLT for a one-day session to determine the professional development needs of the school, again, without consulting the LLT and without the benefit of sustained analysis of student, faculty, and schoolwide data. This meeting focused primarily on teacher perceptions. To add to the confusion, the school's technology team, led by yet another administrator, developed its own professional development plan, which was also completed without any input from the LLT.

To make matters worse, preschool in-service days were structured without providing time for the LLT to present its plan to the faculty. In fact, it was two months before the team was allowed to present, and even then, it was only allowed 15 minutes. By the time the literacy team introduced its initiatives to the faculty, the faculty was already feeling pressured to follow the initiatives set forth by the other professional development plans already in place. Feeling overwhelmed, the faculty viewed the LLT's plan as an additional burden. No attempt was made to link all three initiatives to a common goal of improving student achievement. More importantly, while a considerable amount of professional development was required of teachers, few reasons for the requirements were provided other than compliance.

The structure of determining professional development expectations based on administrative assignments to specific committees led to competition among administrators to be highly successful at their assigned tasks. The result was a fragmented administrative team and faculty. Although each plan was purposeful and valuable, each remained disconnected to a single vision. The LLT, which had spent most of the previous year researching and defining its plan, was frustrated that its hard work was now reduced to a supplementary agenda rather than a guiding vision for schoolwide student achievement improvement.

Situations such as this can occur when there is not a clear understanding of the purpose of the LLT and when there is not a clear schoolwide vision that drives decision making. The goal of creating a shared leadership approach to improving student achievement unraveled into a competitive leadership approach resulting in a lack of vision and focus. No central student achievement focus united the plans, and teachers felt bombarded with initiatives and expectations that appeared to lack connection and which held no common goals.

Referring back to Marzano, Waters, and McNulty's (2005) research on successful leadership characteristics linked to improved student achievement, effective leaders create a school culture founded on a shared vision of the possibilities for what the school can become, develop strong lines of communication to ensure an understanding of the vision, and establish and maintain clear goals and provide clear direction towards achieving those goals. The purpose of the LLT is to support the principal in achieving those goals and to serve as the unifying force to create a collaborative approach focused on improving student achievement. For this to occur, once the LLT has designed the literacy plan, the plan must be shared with the administrative team and must serve as the guiding vision behind all schoolwide initiatives to ensure consistency and relevance. Only one plan can exist for the school. Otherwise, just as demonstrated in the example above, there is little possibility for success.

Summary

Many books have been written addressing the benefits of establishing leadership teams and/or professional learning communities. The research behind the value of such teams is extensive. However, the practical application of developing the teams and ensuring their success is often a mystery. My own experiences working with high-needs schools as they establish and sustain their teams and their plans will serve as the guide for practical implementation. I present not only sound research to support the development of a literacy leadership team, but more importantly, to provide practical means by which to implement and sustain a successful team plan that will guide your school as it works toward achieving its goals.

2

Assembling the Team

Identifying Team Members

Inviting Members

Creating a Collaborative Culture

Choosing the right members for the team is essential if we want the team to run smoothly; therefore, the first step in developing the plan is to carefully assemble the members. An ideal team is comprised of a cross section of effective teacher leaders and administrators.

Identifying Team Members

Effective leaders seek **input** from teachers in the design and implementation of important decisions and policies. The literacy leadership team provides a venue for the principal to gather teachers from different departments and groups to come together as part of the team in designing the literacy plan. Consequently, it is important to think about various functioning teams within the school that need to be represented on the team. For instance, some schools are organized by departments, whereas others are organized by small learning communities or professional learning communities. Make sure the team includes members from all the various factions within the school to insure a balanced input.

The principal's role as **optimizer** is to inspire teachers to become leaders in developing a schoolwide initiative designed to improve student achievement. The principal may choose to work with the reading coach or other members of the school to identify the faculty to include on the team, but ultimately, it is the principal's invitation to join the team that will have the greatest impact. Team members who understand that their time and energies are valued and who believe they are part of a team of individuals committed to finding solutions to school-based issues will tend to devote more to the team than those who join out of pressure or who see this as just another time commitment. This is a great opportunity to provide **affirmation** to the teachers who are working hard, whose students are showing progress, and who are committed to their roles but who tend to quietly close their doors and do their own thing. The principal **optimizer** is always on the lookout for potential leaders who will benefit the school.

At the very least, it is necessary that the team include the principal and the reading coach, if one exists. While I have worked with schools that assign an assistant principal to the team instead of the principal, the most successful schools are those where the principal is a highly **visible** team member. It is also important to maintain a balance of teacher representatives that includes members from each grade level team for elementary schools and members from each of the four academic areas (English, math, social studies, and science) for secondary schools.

What are some of the characteristics of effective team members?

It is also important to carefully select teachers who have demonstrated leadership characteristics. When choosing members for the leadership team, look for those who possess one or more of the following leadership characteristics:

- **Communication:** Teacher leaders who have a strong record of effective communication between other faculty and administrators are vital to the team. Effective communicators will serve as the conduit between the team and the faculty at all stages of planning and implementation.
- **Flexibility:** Look for members who have demonstrated an ability to adapt their behaviors and who encourage others to voice their opinions. The ability to listen to other opinions and a willingness to modify their own agendas is paramount to developing a collegial community.
- **Ideals and Beliefs:** Choose teachers who demonstrate a commitment to students and student learning. Often these are not the most vocal teachers, but they are ones who consistently model best practices in their own classrooms.
- **Optimizer:** Seek out teachers who inspire others and maintain positive attitudes even when under duress.

The goal is to fill the team with highly competent teachers who are recognized by other teachers for their knowledge and skill in the classroom. Find teachers who are successful working with students and teachers; teachers who are admired by other teachers and who are often sought out by other teachers for guidance. Look for those teachers who are approachable and who are known for their willingness to provide guidance and resources to other teachers (Moeller & Pankake, 2006). Identify those teachers who are always finding ways to improve their teaching and who are often quietly engaging their students in active learning.

Some principals make the mistake of assigning department chairs or team leaders to the literacy leadership team. Unfortunately, this often results in undermining the literacy leadership team purpose. Rather than creating a collaborative culture of school-based leaders focused on addressing the literacy needs of the school, literacy often becomes an afterthought to an already overburdened agenda. Many times department chairs are the very members of the school who are overcommitted. They are the "doers" of the school. Adding one more thing for them to do will not ensure commitment to the team. Additionally, simply being a department chair or team leader does not guarantee commitment to improving schoolwide literacy. Department chairs and team leaders often have department-specific agendas that may conflict with the literacy team's purpose. On the other hand, some department chairs and team leaders are excellent resources for the literacy team. The key is to identify those individuals who will best serve the literacy needs of the school.

It is equally important that the team not be comprised of "yes" persons. It is possible for a principal to assemble a "team" that serves merely as the communication link between the principal's initiatives and the faculty. The key to a successful team is to include qualified, committed individuals who are willing to learn together through professional development and research as they collaboratively construct the literacy plan (Lambert, 1998, p. 5).

Although I have worked in some successful schools where membership has been open to the whole faculty, I often found this to be the least successful procedure. Some teachers will join the team because it seems to focus on an issue about which they are curious or perhaps because they know others on the team, but as the commitment to the team becomes more time-consuming, these same teachers often opt out of attendance, leaving a few teachers behind to complete the task. In many cases, the literacy leadership team is originally formed as a volunteer organization, but then changes by the second year to ensure a more committed membership. Helping teachers understand that the literacy leadership team is not simply another school committee will go a long way toward recruiting and retaining committed members.

Some schools also choose to include student and parent representatives. However, take caution when choosing students or parents to become team members. The process of developing a schoolwide initiative is dependent upon the team's ability to engage in thoughtful, reflective dialogue focusing on schoolwide issues. Participants must feel free to express their concerns and observations without fear of offending team members or fear that their thoughts will be repeated beyond the meeting. Some members may not feel comfortable, especially in the early stages of establishing the team culture, with sharing their ideas and concerns when a parent or student is part of the team. I suggest that including students and parents wait until the team has developed a strong community and is able to present the basic concepts of the plan to the faculty.

Inviting Members

One of the most successful ways to assemble your team is to have the principal personally invite members to join. This can be done in several ways. Some schools create personalized written invitations to join the team. In others, the principal personally asks each member to join. Whichever way you choose, be sure to include the following information in the invitation:

- *Remind* them that they have been personally selected to serve on this team because of their past accomplishments as leaders and as effective classroom teachers.

How do I get members to commit to the team?

- *Explain* the time commitment being asked of them. Becoming a member of the literacy leadership team includes more than a commitment to attend monthly meetings. Members might be asked to attend full-day meetings during the school year and during the summers. They might be asked to attend professional development opportunitites that extend beyond the school day.
- *Suggest* to them that membership comes with the responsibility to invest time in team and personal professional development, to implement instructional practices within their own classrooms that have been linked to improved student achievement, to serve as voices of change for the whole school, and to engage in thoughtful, decisive problem solving while working with a team of school leaders.

Creating a Collaborative Culture

Once the team has been assembled, the next goal is to create a collaborative **culture** within the team that will allow for on-going discussion and dialogue revolving around improving student achievement through literacy.

Committees Versus Teams

What's the difference between a committee and a team?

The first order of business is to establish a team approach to membership rather than a committee approach. Teachers and administrators are comfortable attending traditional committee meetings. Meetings might be defined as those times we come together to share information. There is usually an agenda determined by the chair or leader of the meeting. The members' role is to attend the meeting to retrieve the information and perhaps to provide input on a pressing issue. There is no expectation that the member will prepare for the meeting prior to attending the meeting. This is different from establishing a team of individuals who are working together towards a common goal.

We can think of the team concept in terms of a sports team. Each individual on the team has a purpose, a role that is vital to the team's success. To serve that purpose, the team member must prepare for the role through a commitment to attend team meetings, to engage in team practices, and to individually prepare for performance on the team. Athletes who want to play on the team know that their attendance is mandatory and that they will not be allowed to play if they are not present in the preparation for game day.

This concept holds true for the literacy leadership team. Members are expected to attend all meetings, professional development, and commitments planned by the team. They are expected to prepare mentally through their own classroom experiences and through professional development to help create and maintain the team's vision. Members who show up but who do not participate with the team can often become team liabilities.

Dynamic literacy leadership teams (LLTs) understand the team cannot function as a committee, but instead must function as a supportive community of committed individuals. Unlike traditional committee meetings, the LLT doesn't limit itself to meeting once a month on a particular day; rather, it meets as often as needed to accomplish its goals. In the beginning, the team will need sustained time for addressing important issues and developing common goals. Later, once the team has clearly defined goals and expectations, the team meets less often.

Because team meetings are determined by needs, the agenda for the next meeting is set at the end of the previous meeting. Team members are assigned specific tasks to complete before the next meeting and arrive prepared to share their information. The purpose for meeting is to develop a collective vision and action plan to improve student achievement. If this is to truly be a collective process, then team members must partake in the process through data and research collection to support the team's decision-making process. On occasion, teams might meet in response to a crisis or unexpected event, but in most cases, the meetings are well planned and purposeful.

As the team begins the process of creating a collaborative culture, be sure to emphasize the team concept as opposed to the committee concept. Members need to know in advance the type of commitment expected of them in order to prevent future misunderstandings.

Set Aside Time

Finding time to allow the team to become acquainted and begin to develop strong relationships of trust is often difficult but necessary if the members are truly to develop into a team. Again, if we think of this in terms of an athletic team, no team can effectively build a program unless it devotes more time to practice and planning than it does to the game. The same is true for literacy leadership teams.

Schools that only allow for short meetings before or after school will not be as successful as teams that allow for extended team planning. The most successful schools commit to full-day, off-campus meetings. Ideally, this would include two or three days off campus at the early stages of team development in order to build relationships within the team, create a vision for the team, identify areas of concern, and begin the process of professional development in order to determine the best interventions. For some schools, these meetings might take place in the spring or summer prior to the next school year. For others, it might mean taking time during the fall semester to develop the plan. Once the plan has been established, the team should meet at least quarterly to determine the plan's effectiveness and to discuss possible changes.

Finding the necessary **resources** to provide time for planning can be difficult. Some schools hire substitutes for teachers to attend the meetings during the school day. One particular school I worked with arranged for substitutes for teachers to attend three, full-day planning sessions off-campus. They chose an off-campus site in order to guarantee few interruptions for either the teachers or the administrators. These meetings were scheduled throughout the fall semester. Other schools have chosen to have the team meet prior to the beginning of school for either one or two days to develop the plan and then meet monthly throughout the school year. They then schedule an additional full-day planning session late in the school year to assess their progress and begin planning for the next year. Allotting time for the team to work together to develop a well-researched plan that is applicable to your school site is essential. Schools that rush to devise a plan are often frustrated with the lack of success.

I have a friend who is always telling me that the growth is in the conversation. If that is the case, then it becomes paramount that the next order of business is to begin establishing a culture of conversation. To accomplish this, the first team planning session needs to begin with time to develop relationships as a means of setting the expectation that we are all on the team as equals who are individually and collectively valued.

Get Acquainted

How do we begin the conversations?

I suggest you begin with an icebreaker, an opportunity for the participants to get to know each other on a personal level. The goal is to provide a safe environment for the members to become acquainted while at the same time establishing a sense of community.

- A very basic icebreaker is to simply ask the members to share their names, their current positions, and their goal as a member of the team. While this may be a time saver, it may result in superficial introductions and does not allow for members to begin to develop relationships.
- One of my favorite methods is to prepare signs in advance that have pictures of the various parts of a car. Place these signs throughout the room. Ask the participants to think of the team as the "driving force" behind positive changes at the school. Suggest to them that for a car to run smoothly, all parts of the car must be in working order. It is the sum of the parts that guarantees the successful running of the car. Ask them to think about their own personalities and strengths. What part of the car do they most identify with and why? Parts to include might be:
  - **Engine.** Everything stops when the engine breaks down. These are the "doers" in the room, the people who see the project through to completion.
  - **Tires.** Without tires, the road is bumpy and dangerous. These are the people who are looking out for possible road hazards. They are able to predict possible resistance to the plan and provide alternative solutions.
  - **Ignition.** The car goes no where unless the ignition is working. These are the people who have ideas and who are always excited about beginning the new project. They have a plan in mind and know where the car should be going. They provide a purpose for the travel. Often they are not the best ones to sustain the drive because they find themselves planning the next trip while others are still working on finishing the first one.
  - **Bumper.** How many times have your bumpers protected your car from serious damage? Bumper people can smooth ruffled feathers and provide reasons for the plan when others are resisting. They are good at helping others buy into the plan while protecting the plan from destruction.
  - **Doors.** Doors allow people to enter and leave the car. Some people are especially good at finding the right people who are willing to join the team, and they are terrific at making new people feel welcome.

- **Headlights.** Headlights guide us through the fog or the darkness. Headlight people are problem solvers. They look for solutions. They also are willing to do the research, to look for possibilities.

The next step is to give the participants time to identify the part that best defines their strengths and to meet with others in the room who identify with the same part. Allow time for them to talk about why they identify with that part and then share out with the whole group.

This approach allows members to talk with others about the individual strengths they bring to the team as they begin to develop more personal relationships. It also serves to remind the team that each member plays an essential role in developing and maintaining the team goals and that while each member's area of expertise may differ from that of other members, each is vital to the whole team.

- Another way of allowing members to get acquainted and begin to activate their prior knowledge about literacy is to prepare note cards in advance with words directly related to literacy. For example, you might have note cards with the following words written on them: *literacy, progress monitoring, content-area literacy, standardized tests, reciprocal teaching, leveled text, data-driven instruction, differentiated instruction, modeling, engagement,* and *direct instruction.* Pass out one card to each person and ask members to move about the room encountering people they do not know. As they meet each new person, they should introduce themselves and each share the word or phrase on the card and discuss what they think this means. Time should be allotted at the end of the activity for whole-group discussion.

There are, of course, lots of other ways to get the members up, moving, and interacting with each other. Use the one that best fits your audience.

Setting Team Protocols

Many times we assume that everyone is a professional and will automatically follow expected protocols. However, I have found it quite useful to spend time allowing the team to develop its own set of protocols that will guide future team meetings. Establishing clear guidelines enables the team to function in an **orderly** fashion. This allows the team members to develop relationships and secure a sense of ownership as they work together to establish a supportive culture. It is a safe way to introduce the concept that everyone is involved in the decision-making process.

This can be done in a variety of ways. Some schools simply chart ideas and then collectively choose the ones they believe are essential. Others use small groups to discuss the protocols they believe are necessary and then share out. This allows all members to participate and is very helpful at the beginning when members are still developing the team culture. Members who feel intimidated or cautious might feel more comfortable working with a partner to identify team protocols they deem necessary rather than first sharing out with the whole team. Ultimately, the team needs to reach consensus about team expectations for member's behavior.

How do we establish a "purposeful community"?

Some teams are quite creative while others are more straight-forward in their creation. Once the protocols have been established, it is a good idea to begin each planning session with a review. The following are examples of team protocols developed by schools in Florida:

LAFFS: *L*istening with deeper understanding. *A*ttitude (positive, acceptance, and respect). *F*lexibility. *F*ocus (goals, time, conversations). *S*mall baby steps (snail steps).

BARS: *B*e supportive. *A*ctively listen. *R*espect others' opinions. *S*afe environment.

CBS: *C*ommitment. *B*e professional. *S*tudents First.

Setting Team Purpose

Once your team has had time to get acquainted and to establish the team protocols, it's time to begin the more serious discussion of the team's purpose. It is at this point that the principal begins to outline his or her **ideals and beliefs** for the team outcomes. The purpose here is to remind the team that they have been individually selected for their various strengths and to reinforce the principal's belief that they can work together to identify and solve important issues affecting the school.

Although it may seem like a good time to delve into the data and issues impacting the school, remember that at this point we are still establishing relationships and defining our purpose. Instead, this is a good time to begin discussions about the team's vision for the school, their understanding of literacy and how it impacts curriculum, and their own perceptions of issues that should be addressed. I suggest that time be allowed for the team to discuss these three concepts at length. The most successful way to address this is to allow time for the team to work in small groups for more personal conversation followed by whole group sharing and discussion leading to consensus.

- **Vision:** Eaker, Dufour, and Dufour (2002) suggest the first conversation should focus on the school's vision. Ask the team to discuss the following questions:
  - Why do we exist as a school?
  - What kind of school do we hope to become?
  - How must we behave in order to create the kind of school we hope to become?
- **Literacy:** Providing an opportunity for the team to discuss what it means to be literate, especially as it relates to their own individual content area, is another topic for rich discussion. Asking members to consider what it means to be a literate scientist versus a literate mathematician or how reading literature is different from reading historical text is an important concept to examine early on in developing team goals. Questions to consider include:
  - What does it mean to be literate in my content area?
  - What skills must students demonstrate to become literate in my content area?
  - How might my instruction need to change in order to prepare students to be literate in my content area?
- **Issues:** Finally, allowing the team time to brainstorm issues they believe are paramount to improving student achievement provides vital information relating to member perceptions. The issues raised by the team are probably the same issues others on the faculty have discussed. Allowing time for the team to discuss and prioritize these issues will provide guidance and direction for the next steps. Suggestions include:
  - What are the primary issues impeding students from understanding my content?
  - What needs to change in order for students to be successful in my classroom?

Conclusion

There is a tendency for some schools to skip the process of creating a team **culture** and identifying a collective vision for team purpose. As educators, our instinct is to begin immediately with the problem solving process. Unfortunately, when we begin providing solutions without taking the time to understand the problem and all its implications, we often end up spinning our wheels.

Some will argue that community building just takes too much time. However, I strongly urge your team to take the time to establish relationships and define expectations prior to looking for solutions. The team is expected to function as a collaborative group working towards a common goal. Establishing a strong team culture while building consensus about the team's purpose and vision will go a long way toward successfully designing and implementing the team plan.

3

Collecting and Analyzing Data

High-Stakes Testing Data

Additional Data Sources

Triangulating Data

Data Conversations

Once the team is established, it is time to begin the process of identifying the key factors necessary to accomplish the overall team goal of improving student achievement. Keeping in mind the foundational elements: student achievement, research, and professional development, when we think about data collection we must also consider the sources of data that will provide us with insight for each of these elements. We collect student data to identify areas of concern relating to improving student achievement. We collect teacher data to identify areas of concern relating to instructional practices. We then narrow our focus to identify specific areas of concern relating to both students and teachers to identify specific research needed to help us design a successful plan.

The first step is for the team to begin analyzing data from multiple sources. Some schools tend to rush into problem solving rather than spend time investigating the source of the problem. Rarely does this approach result in positive outcomes. Instead, rushing into quick solutions often results in a continuous cycle of initiating new programs that are quickly abandoned, leading to frustration by teachers and students. The ultimate goal of the literacy leadership team is to develop and support lasting change, a course of action that requires time, investigation, and reflection. Careful analysis of data guides the decision-making process and provides support for initiatives.

Think of team sports. Successful teams spend a lot of time reviewing team films, looking at plays that didn't work, and identifying exactly where the game plan broke down. They also look at what is working well and build on successful plays. Successful teams spend a lot of time analyzing and reflecting on past performances and current resources before determining the course of action.

High-Stakes Testing Data

We exist in a data-intense environment. High-stakes student assessments are reported through the media and used by politicians to change education policy; used by parents to choose schools for their children; used by district and school-based administrators to identify struggling students and to determine class schedules; and the list goes on. Ultimately, one would be hard-pressed to go through a week without having access to some form of student assessment data. Unfortunately, the current emphasis on high-stakes testing tends to overemphasize state-mandated testing data while ignoring school-based data. Having said that, our purpose is not to ignore the high-stakes testing data, but rather to find ways to more effectively analyze such data.

How do we know what the data means?

Determining Purpose

Our first step is to determine the purpose of the data. According to Brenner, Pearson, and Rief (2007, p. 260), data collection provides information in four essential categories: (a) communicating with students concerning their achievement, (b) designing and assessing curriculum, (c) communicating with outside audiences such as families and administrators, and (d) comparing student performances between groups, classes, schools, districts, states, etc. Most high-stakes testing data function effectively as a means of assessing student achievement, communicating with outside audiences, and comparing performances. Unfortunately, they are not particularly useful in designing and assessing curriculum. Our goal as a team is to gather additional data that will help us to design a plan that brings about successful changes in curriculum and that ultimately impacts student performance on high-stakes tests.

Summative Data

High-stakes testing data are summative in nature. They provide a "snapshot" of student achievement at a given point in time. Many schools and districts, as well as the general public, make the mistake of determining success based solely on these yearly reports. This results in many problems. First, because most high-stakes testing is given only once a year, we have no way of determining whether or not our initiatives and interventions are impacting student achievement during the course of the year. Second, we are not testing the same students each year. Instead we are testing a new set of students who bring with them different backgrounds and experiences. Again, we have no way of determining whether or not the scores are reflective of our instructional practices and interventions or are a result of changes in student population.

Thinking back to the team sports analogy, consider this. If a team does poorly in the state finals one year but does extremely well the next year, we celebrate the team's success. However, if the new team is made up of entirely new players, we cannot say for certain that the success was as a result of either the coaches or of changes in their coaching practices. It might be entirely a result of the new set of team players. The same is true for high-stakes testing.

Finally, the yearly data provided by high-stakes testing neither provides an understanding of the causes for student achievement (either high or low) nor an understanding of curriculum effectiveness. Additionally, correlating high-stakes testing data to individual teacher performance is nearly impossible because of the comprehensive nature of the tests. They provide little guidance for determining which interventions might improve student achievement or which professional development might improve instruction.

On a good note, many states are now examining and reporting student developmental scores which measure individual student improvement on the same set of skills from year to year. These scores are more useful in determining the impact of schoolwide initiatives and interventions, but they are not good indicators of individual teacher impact. Once again, they provide summative data that will help us determine whether or not our initiatives are effective; however, they should not be the sole source of information for determining which factors are having the most significant impact on student achievement.

Norm-Referenced Versus Criterion-Referenced Data

What is the difference between norm referenced and criterion referenced?

When analyzing data it is equally important to determine whether the test scores are norm referenced or criterion referenced. Norm-referenced tests are determined by placing the average of all student scores across a bell curve. The majority of scores fall within the average range with a few scores falling either above average or below average. The resulting scores reflect the individual student's score in relationship to the scores of a given population. Norm-referenced scores are not useful in determining the effectiveness of curriculum or instruction. Their strength is in helping us make comparisons across student populations.

Criterion-referenced tests measure student achievement on specific skills. Student scores are determined by their mastery of the content and not in relationship to how others did on the test. These scores are more effective in determining the impact of curriculum and instruction because they are more closely aligned to the curriculum; however, year-to-year scores are still dependent on the population being tested and, consequently, are not specific enough to determine whether it was the curriculum or the students who are responsible for changes in achievement.

Analyzing High-Stakes Testing Data

Recognizing the limitation of relying on high-stakes testing is the starting point for effective use of these data. The next step is to begin a careful analysis. These data are very useful for identifying areas of concern that need to be addressed. For example, a school might find that 53% of their students scored below grade level on state-mandated reading assessments, suggesting a need to improve student reading achievement. The data provide a focus for further investigation by indicating an area of concern but do not provide significant information to determine why students are performing below grade level. The team needs more information before developing a plan to raise student reading achievement.

Longitudinal Data

One step toward analyzing these data more effectively includes examining longitudinal data. Reviewing longitudinal data provides a picture of student achievement over time. Is there evidence that student achievement is improving over time, declining over time, or stagnant over time? These data can help us begin to look for trends and identify potential causes.

How can we best use high stakes data to focus on areas of concern?

One school examined their longitudinal data and noted a steady decline over several years that could be traced back to school redistricting. When they compared their student achievement scores over time to their changing demographics over years, they were able to make a link between achievement and changes in student population.

However, we must be cautious about jumping to conclusions based on simple year-to-year data. For example, I worked with two high schools in the same district that had changed their student schedules from a block format to a seven-period-day format. Both schools noted a significant change in student writing scores on the state-mandated writing exam. One school attributed its increase to the new seven-period day, whereas the other school attributed its decrease to the new seven-period day. Neither considered the impact of the changing student population or differences in instructional practices. Clearly, both schools would have benefited from additional data to more effectively identify the reason for the changing scores.

Disaggregated Data

Another step is to disaggregate the data to identify specific population differences in achievement. Looking beyond the whole-school data to examine individual population differences provides a clearer picture of areas of concern. However, it is equally important that schools do not allow disaggregated data to reinforce bias against certain groups. Simply acknowledging that one group of students performs lower than another does not indicate why this happens. If the majority of these students are denied access to rigorous course work, their low performance may be a result of curriculum and not ethnicity. We must always keep in mind that the data merely indicates a concern but does not report a cause (Johnson, 2002). Misused disaggregated data can lead some teachers to conclude they are not responsible for improving student achievement for groups who traditionally score lower than other groups. Remember, the goal of disaggregated data is to highlight the need to further investigate ways to improve student achievement for all students.

Disaggregating student data can also eliminate some of the assumptions that often impede effective interventions. One high school concerned with its low reading scores made the assumption that English-language-learner (ELL) students were pulling down the school's grade. The school spent a good portion of the year asking for help from the district to provide professional development to help teachers work with ELL students. Toward the end of the year, while addressing a different issue, the school discovered that only 7% of its total population was made up of ELL students. Because its entire literacy plan was based on faulty assumptions, few to no interventions were implemented for the remaining 93% of the student population.

Effective analysis of high-stakes testing data must include a combination of longitudinal and disaggregated data. Successful teams use high-stakes testing data as a starting point, an indicator for an area of concern that will benefit from further analysis. These data should never be used as the sole resource for establishing a schoolwide plan; however, combining longitudinal and disaggregated high-stakes testing data can serve as a means of helping the team focus on the most essential areas of concern.

Additional Data Sources

Once we have identified an area of concern based on high-stakes testing data, we are now ready to begin examining reasons why this concern exists. Human nature leads us to conclude that there must be reasons other than our own teaching that explain poor student performance. It is not unusual for teams to begin the process of explaining away poor student performance by blaming students, parents, society, or lack of resources. Unfortunately, as long as we continue to place responsibility for achievement solely on the shoulders of our most struggling students without accepting responsibility for changing instructional practices, we eliminate need for school reform (Urdan & Schoenfelder, 2006). The best way to counter these assumptions is to begin to examine data beyond high-stakes tests so that we are collecting input from all members of the school community.

Ultimately, when we begin to focus our data collection beyond high-stakes testing we begin the process of creating an inquiry-based collaborative team approach to identifying and solving school-based issues. We create community rather than reinforce divisions. We are establishing communication between all interested parties and focusing on problem solving rather than blame placing. We are changing the traditional process of top-down decision making to collaborative decision making.

Let's begin with an example from an alternative middle school. When the team met to discuss their school's scores and identify possible ways to improve student achievement, the faculty overwhelmingly began to place blame on the students. Teachers complained that students did not turn in their homework and came to class unprepared. Rather than admonish the faculty for their assumptions, the very wise reading coach suggested they do some action research to determine the pervasiveness of the problem.

Each teacher agreed to collect weekly data for one month. On random days and during random periods determined by the team, each teacher counted the number of students who came to class with their homework completed and with all their supplies so they could begin to work. The data were reported to the reading coach at the end of the month and presented at the next literacy leadership team. Much to their surprise, the team discovered that 67% of their students arrived in class with their homework completed, and 80% had their supplies.

What other forms of data will guide our decision-making process?

The coach was successful in guiding her team toward examining other options by validating their concerns and suggesting they collect data to confirm their ideas. Originally, this team began with the state-mandated data and rushed to identify the problem by making assumptions. However, rather than proceed with their assumption, the team agreed to collect data to validate their concerns. Upon learning that a majority of the students did come to class prepared and did complete their homework, the team's next step was to reconsider their plan. Part of that plan included a need to further examine the type and amount of homework assigned in each class. At each step of the process, the team focused on school-based data to make decisions about their next step.

Schools are rich in uncollected data that can be used to more effectively determine possible courses of action. Much of this data can be collected informally through observation and survey. Allow time for the team to think about and discuss alternative data sources available to them.

Student Data

Student data is often the easiest to collect. Frequently schools collect and report student achievement scores, class grades, ethnicity, socioeconomic status, and other data. However, many schools stop at the reporting phase rather than moving forward to the analysis phase. Examining student data in conjunction with other data will help the team make appropriate decisions that will lead to improved student achievement.

Some additional student data sources to consider are:

- *Attendance:* Comparing student attendance rates to student achievement scores is one way to identify specific students to target. Although conventional wisdom might lead us to expect that low-performing students are absent more often than high-performing students, this might not be the case. We can also examine the link between attendance and class. Which classes do students miss most often? What is the cause of most absences? Are students skipping? Is it caused by transportation issues? Some schools have adopted special transportation options for students who miss school for reasons beyond their control. If attendance is a problem, we need to be asking ourselves, "What can we do about it to help students achieve?"
- *Discipline Records:* Student misbehavior can also be attributed to many factors. Collecting discipline records to identify which students miss class most often can help us to establish interventions. However, we need to examine the issue beyond mere data collection of student names. We want to determine the causes for student misbehavior and find ways to eliminate the behaviors as a way to improve student success. Some questions to consider include:
    - Are these students missing all classes or just one in particular?
    - Do these students cause problems for one teacher but not for others?
    - Are some teachers reporting more discipline issues than others?
    - Is discipline addressed consistently throughout the school?
- *District Progress Monitoring Data:* Some schools and districts collect specific progress monitoring data such as fluency scores and standards assessments. Data focusing on specific skills can be particularly useful for determining the effectiveness of curricular interventions. One middle school examined its students' flu-

ency scores and noted that students' scores were not improving over the course of the year. The team used that data to plan for professional development to help teachers understand fluency and its connection to comprehension and to learn how to incorporate fluency instruction within the content areas. Skill-based progress monitoring is very useful for identifying specific instructional changes that need to be addressed and for determining the effectiveness of the interventions.

- *Student Perceptions:* One of the least used data sources is asking students what they think. Some schools bring a group of students together to talk about issues the students feel are important to their success. Other schools survey students to find out what they know about an issue or what they would like to see happen. They ask students how they feel about initiatives or programs adopted by the school. They interview students from all ethnic groups, socioeconomic levels, grade levels, etc., in order to assess student perceptions. They then use this data when making decisions. Appendix A is an example of a student survey used to identify which literacy strategies they knew and used on a regular basis.

There are, of course, multiple other student data sources that might be pertinent to your school. The key is to identify student data that will help your team make good decisions and set priorities.

Teacher Data

Collecting teacher data is equally important when trying to determine the best course of action. However, caution must be exercised to maintain teacher privacy. Although we want to encourage teachers to collect progress monitoring data and initiate action research within their own classrooms, as a literacy team we need to remember that our goal is to identify specific areas of concern that impact the whole school. We must be careful that we don't overstep our boundaries and begin to analyze individual teacher performance. Therefore, it is best that the team focus on "frequency data" as a means of determining priorities rather than look at specific teacher data. Individual teacher data should only be collected by administrators and kept in complete confidentiality. There are, however, many ways to collect teacher frequency data which can be used to design your plan.

- *Teacher Surveys:* Just as with students, it is important to ask teachers about their perceptions of the problems and issues surrounding the school. Teacher surveys can be used to determine the effectiveness of program initiatives, determine teacher knowledge of instructional practices, and identify teacher needs. The most successful schools collect teacher surveys during regularly scheduled faculty meetings. Surveys left in teachers' boxes tend to be misplaced and rarely make it back to the collection box. Some schools use computer-based survey programs that allow them to issue the surveys electronically. These programs also provide analysis of the results and printouts that can be used for discussion. Appendix B is a sample of a teacher survey used to collect literacy instructional practice information.

- *Administrative Walk-Through Data:* One of the most effective ways to collect instructional practice data is through the administrative walk-through. As administrators visit classrooms throughout the month, they collect data relevant to the literacy plan. They make note of the types of instructional practices they are observing and the percentage of the time they observe these practices. For instance, a principal might report that during 50 visits over the period of one month, 85% of the time teachers were engaged in lecture. This type of frequency data can then be reported back to the team to identify teacher needs and plan effectiveness.
- *Professional Development Data:* Collecting data indicating the types of professional development teachers are attending along with the percentage of teachers who are engaging in the professional development is also useful data for guiding the planning. If one of the schoolwide initiatives involves increasing the amount of time teachers incorporate literacy instruction in classrooms, it becomes important to identify how many teachers have received the proper professional development to enable them to accomplish the goal. This could even go further to determine whether or not a particular professional development translated into changes in instructional practice.

When determining which data to collect, it is important to remember our goal. Needless data collection results in frustration for both the staff and the team. The idea is to collect data that will provide insight into identified areas of concern. The most important part of the data collection is the analysis and reflection to determine a course of action. Ultimately, it's what we do with the data that determines the success or failure of our school goals.

Triangulating Data

When using data to make informed decisions it is always best to collect data from at least two or three different resources. As mentioned earlier, it is easy to draw conclusions about data that may prove incorrect upon closer examination. Collecting data from different sources allows us to compare the results to see if they are in agreement or disagreement with our original idea.

Why is triangulation important?

For example, a student may perform poorly on a state-mandated test, but a review of the student's grade might indicate the student has been successful in most of his classes. Additional data needs to be collected to determine whether or not the student's performance on the state test was a true measure of the student's ability. We might choose to conference with the student to determine the student's perception of the test. We might also choose to have the student take a diagnostic test to look more closely at the student's performance on the standards being tested. Finally, we might also look at some of the student's classwork and compare it to the standards being tested. If all four of these indicators suggest that the student has met mastery of the standard, then our intervention will focus on test-taking strategies and conferencing. If, however, we find that the student's grades were high, but the student's work and diagnostic tests reveal a need for further instruction to address the standard, then our intervention will focus on providing the student with additional instruction to improve achievement.

Real-World Example

A small K-8 magnet school of the arts formed a literacy leadership team to try to figure out how to meet the needs of its students. The school's students were primarily low-socioeconomic students from a transient population. The literacy leadership team noted that the school's teachers had received multiple professional development opportunities focusing on incorporating literacy strategy instruction in all classrooms. However, they also noted that student scores were not improving.

The team established two subcommittees to write surveys: one for teachers and one for students. They wanted to know if teachers were implementing the strategies in the classroom and if students were using them. Once the surveys were completed and approved by the team, the teachers were given the surveys. Overwhelmingly teachers reported they were incorporating the strategies in classrooms. A few weeks later, the team gave the surveys to students. Students reported they didn't know what the strategies were and rarely used them. In the meantime, the administrative team agreed to conduct walk-throughs to collect data to determine the type of instruction observed in most classrooms. After one month, the administrative team reported that 90% of the time teachers were observed giving lectures.

The team now had significant data to indicate that while teachers had received specific professional development focusing on literacy strategies, students rarely used the strategies. More importantly, the administrative data indicated that students had little time to practice the strategies even if they were being taught strategies because most of the instruction was provided through lecture. Recognizing that students needed to be working in small groups so teachers could provide guided practice using the strategies, the team decided to focus on small-group instruction for the coming year. Teachers were provided with additional professional development. The reading coaches modeled managing small-group instruction and coached teachers to help them implement small groups in all classrooms. The administrative team set expectations for small-group instruction and continued to complete walk-throughs while regularly reporting their data to the whole school.

Two years later, the school reported an increase in the amount of small-group instruction and student use of literacy strategies. The school reported that student reading scores had improved and for the first time, the school met AYP (adequate yearly progress) for all students. The school largely attribute its success to identifying a specific problem, narrowing the school's focus on instruction, providing professional development to change instruction, and setting clear expectations for the whole school.

Data Conversations

Successful teams do not begin with a plan in mind but rather with a goal of identifying a plan that best serves the community. Teams must be allowed substantial time to work as a professional community to examine school data, to identify specific school needs, to develop an action plan, and to continually collect data to reflect on the plan's progress.

Collecting data and preparing it for the team meeting is a lengthy process and must be completed outside the team meeting. Administrators can take the lead by taking charge of data collection. Some schools are fortunate to have a data subcommittee that collects the data for presentation. Other times it is the reading coach's responsibility to collect the data. Whatever the process, it is vital that the data is collected and reported regularly.

Allowing significant time for the team to analyze data and discuss its implications is equally important. We must be careful that we don't allow the person or people collecting the data to become the driving force behind the decision making. The data is only one step in developing an effective plan. If members of the team feel they are merely attending meetings to approve or disapprove of initiatives defined by others, the team will soon fall apart.

Begin with the obvious high stakes testing data. Provide time for discussion to allow for input from the whole team reflecting their ideas on what the data suggest. The following chart can be used to guide the discussion surrounding data.

- Using chart paper, write the following topics on the paper: *Area of Concern; Existing Data Supporting the Concern; Additional Information Needed* (see Figure 3.1).

Figure 3.1. Discussion Guide

Area of Concern	Existing Data Supporting the Concern	Additional Information Needed
Based on what you already know, what is your biggest concern relating to student achievement?	What data have you already collected that supports this as an area of concern?	What additional data do you need to triangulate your conclusion? Who is responsible for collecting that data? When will the data be collected?

- Allow time for members to talk with table partners to express their own ideas relating to each topic before opening the discussion to the whole team. This insures that each person has an opportunity for input in the process.
- Chart all responses and allow time for discussion leading to consensus.
- Validate team members' concerns and ideas with further research or discussion
- Identify additional research that needs to be conducted and set up committees to begin the process.
- Set time limits for data collection and reporting.

The process of collecting, reviewing, and analyzing the data can be lengthy, depending on the availability of data. In some cases, time must be allowed to collect additional data to validate conclusions. However, careful analysis of data prior to establishing a plan will go a long way toward ensuring success.

Once the team is satisfied it has significant data to make informed decisions, it is now ready to begin developing the plan.

4

Developing the Plan

A careful review of the data often indicates specific student and teacher needs. However, the data is not sufficient for designing a successful plan. Now is the time for the team to examine the research linked to improving student achievement. Remember that the data provides us with an awareness of what needs to be addressed, but it does not provide us with the solution. Think back to the foundational elements: student achievement, instructional practices, and research. Now is the time to engage in research to identify possible solutions to the areas of concern identified in the data.

Schools that rush into goal setting without the support of additional research may discover at the end of the year that their goals were not met. Setting goals without an action plan for changing the outcome results in failure. One such illustration occurred when a school devised a plan with the goal of increasing the percentage of students making gains on the state reading exam by 5% for both whole-school data and subgroup data. This goal reflected the student data from the previous year but did not indicate specific changes in curriculum or instruction that would impact student learning, nor did it provide for collection of assessment data throughout the year to determine whether or not the school was making progress towards achieving its goal

When we met in the spring to plan for the following year, we had no data to determine the plan's success because it was solely dependent on scores from state exams. Unfortunately, this example is similar to many of the school improvement plans I review each year. The school keeps adjusting the percentage of students they hope improve achievement, but they don't provide any specific plan for achieving that goal.

Effective plans are the result of collaboration by a community of dedicated faculty and staff willing to spend the time and energy to study the problem, identify specific interventions, practice the interventions in their own classrooms, and develop a plan for professional development to support and encourage schoolwide implementation of the changes. Thus, effective literacy teams serve as collaborative professional learning communities focused on investigating and implementing possible interventions. Teams engaging in these practices tend to be more successful than teams that do not (Eaker, DuFour, & DuFour, 2002; Joyce & Showers, 2002, Marzano, Waters, & McNulty, 2005). Identifying the specific intervention that will work best for the school's faculty and students requires careful consideration if the team is to develop a plan that results in lasting curricular and instructional changes impacting student learning.

Keeping the goal in mind, the leadership team serves as the foundation for educational reform at the school, which means that members of the team must be willing to engage in sustained professional development focusing on improving student learning within their own classrooms. I often remind teams not to impose curriculum changes and professional development requirements on staff that they themselves are unwilling to incorporate. A wise teacher once told me that teachers need to understand the "compelling why" before they are willing to change their instruction. As the team goes through the process of examining student data and researching best practices followed by implementing these same practices in their own classrooms, they will develop their own sense of why these changes are important and how they improve not only student learning but instructional practices as well. The team then becomes the model for effective change in the classroom.

Reviewing the Research

A first step in determining the best course of action is to research and discuss characteristics of effective instruction and identify those practices that will best serve the needs of the school. Prior to making permanent decisions, the team must engage in **intellectual stimulation** by reviewing current research and theories relevant to their school needs and take time to engage in thoughtful discussion. I suggest schools begin with research focusing on best practices for improving student achievement and then narrow their study to specific interventions addressing specific instructional needs after they have an understanding of the big picture. *Creating Literacy-Rich Schools for Adolescents* (Ivey & Fisher, 2006) and *Reading Next: A Vision for Action and Research in Middle and High School Literacy* (Biancarosa & Snow, 2006; available online as well as in print) are excellent resources for identifying specific characteristics of successful schools. Additional current research linked to improved student literacy achievement can be found on the Internet, in professional journals, and in professional books. Appendix C provides a suggested list of resources.

Analyzing Research Within the Team

Facilitating discussion of the research is paramount to a team's success. Although time constraints often lead us to consider passing out articles to members and asking them to read the information and report back to the team at the next meeting, this format is rarely successful. In many cases, a majority of the members do not read the paper prior to the meeting, resulting in limited conversation and frustration. The facilitator is then forced to summarize the information and, essentially, to make the decision for the team rather than have the team make the decision collectively. Instead, plan time for the team to meet, read, and discuss the research together.

Engaging the team in serious discussion of research does not just happen. The prudent facilitator takes care to implement well-defined guided discussion that ensures all members have time to read and think about the research, time to talk about the research with other team members in a safe environment that encourages full participation, and time to identify best practices that meet the needs of the school. The key is to guide the discussion process while being careful not to influence the discussion outcome. Remember that the power is in the conversation.

How do I engage members in critical analysis and discussion?

The following activities are useful for guiding discussion.

- *Activate Prior Knowledge:* Begin each session with a brainstorming activity addressing the specific issues or concerns to be addressed. For example, when studying *Creating Literacy-Rich Schools for Adolescents,* I begin the discussion by asking the team to consider Ivey and Fisher's (2006) initial question, "What does it mean to be literate?" (p. xiii) I allow time for members to think about this question in relation to their own content and then chart their responses. After the members have shared, I ask them to read the introduction and highlight important details as they think about how the book confirms or contradicts their original responses to the brainstorming question.
- *Read Selected Sections:* Sometimes it is unnecessary for the team to read the entire document. Skillful facilitators identify key sections of the text for the whole team to read. When examining *Reading Next: A Vision for Action and Research in Middle and High School Literacy* (Biancarosa & Snow, 2006), rather than have the team read the whole document during the meeting, I break the document into sections. We begin by reading the introduction and highlighting key elements that each member finds interesting, alarming, or confusing. After they finish reading, I chart their responses and provide a brief overview of the research and essential elements necessary to understand the research. This is then followed by a jigsaw activity.
- *Jigsaw the Text:* Lengthy text can also be divided into sections that can be read by small groups within the team. Breaking the team into small groups encourages more timid members to en-

gage in serious discussion and provides a safe environment in which to share concerns and ideas. When studying the *Reading Next* document, I divide the team into groups of two to three members and assign each group two or three of the "Fifteen Elements of Effective Adolescent Literacy Programs" (Biancarosa & Snow, 2006, pp. 4–5) identified in the document to read and discuss. After allowing time for discussion, each group shares its understanding of the elements and how each element might be implemented or might impact their school. Whenever possible, I provide chart paper for teams to chart their ideas and use when they are sharing with the whole group.

- *Element Charts:* Many texts are organized around key points, factors, elements, and the like, as defined by the research. For example, Ivey and Fisher (2006) identify five areas impacting secondary literacy: English language arts classes; content-area classes; sustained silent reading/independent reading; intervention and support for struggling readers; and leadership and schoolwide support. They provide quality indicator rubrics for each area. One activity is to have the team review each of these indicators and use highlighters to determine whether or not they believe the areas are important and identify which indicators are evident in the school environment. Once members have completed the activity, lead the team in a discussion of which indicators are essential to begin the change process at your school.

  Another example is to create a chart that includes key factors from the research and ask participants to define their own perception of the level of importance for each element and whether or not they believe there is evidence in the school to suggest the element is, in fact, already being addressed. For example, after discussing the 15 elements from the *Reading Next* document, I ask the members to complete an Element Chart (see Appendix D) as a way for them to think about the elements and identify those they believe will best serve the needs of their school. The purpose of these charts is to help teams make connections between research, theory, and practice to the school environment while generating discussion focusing on how the research impacts their individual school needs. An added activity for follow-up is to have the team members take these charts and rubrics back to their individual departments and ask the departments to complete the same process. They then bring the results back to the team. This allows the team to collect input from the whole school and often leads to clearer pictures of the state of the school.

Guiding the team through the discussion process using some or all of the activities listed above can be modified for any research article or book study. The key is for the facilitator to read the text in advance of the meeting and create a plan for the discussion. Simply handing the text to the team at the beginning of the meeting without a plan often results in unfocused discussion. Leading the team through the steps for critical reading and discussion produces better results.

Narrowing the Focus

Once the team is confident it has a good understanding of the specific needs of the school and is comfortable with the research linking curricular and instructional changes to improving student achievement, it is now ready to develop an action plan. One mistake many schools make is trying to implement too many changes at one time. I find it useful to adhere to the advice from the *Reading Next* (Biancarosa & Snow, 2006) document and identify one or two instructional changes along with one infrastructural change designed to support the instructional change. The idea is to identify one or two instructional practices that teachers can implement in their classrooms while at the same time begin the process of changing the school culture to one focused on a common goal of improving student achievement. For example, if the school goal is to improve literacy instruction in content-area classrooms, then the infrastructural goal might include establishing teacher teams to investigate means for embedding effective instructional principles in all content areas. This differs from the generalized goal of improving reading achievement for all students.

How do we determine our focus?

Now that the team has now identified a specific instructional goal, as well as one means of implementing that goal, conversations should focus on identifying specific professional development to present to the whole staff as starting point for initiating change.

Care must be taken not to "railroad" potential changes through the planning process. Frequently, teams are dominated by vocal individuals who come to the team with their own agendas and plans. This often results in insincere compliance from less-dominant team members who leave the meeting feeling frustrated. One such example is a high school that decided to implement a "one book, one school" initiative to raise literacy awareness by having the whole school read the same book. One team member tried to voice his concerns, but the team generally ignored him and proceeded with its plan. Once the plan was taken to the whole school, the dissenting member took pains to let the faculty know that he did not support this initiative. The team found itself spending a lot of time defending its position. Ultimately, the principal had to step in and reinforce his support for the team. Had the team taken time to hear the dissenting member's concerns and acknowledged that others on the faculty might have the same concerns, they could have been prepared for possible objections and planned for ways to address those needs. Instead they found themselves having to promote the plan to a divided faculty.

Developing consensus and limiting schoolwide initiatives to those areas the whole team can support is essential for success. Divided teams yield divided faculties. Wise facilitators provide time to hear all members' concerns and guide the team in reaching consensus. This can be accomplished through various activities.

- *Charts and Dots:* One way to counter this outcome is to chart the major ideas developed during discussion and provide members with a specific number of dots (I usually limit the number of dots to three or four) to place next to the ideas they believe are most important or that will have the greatest impact on the school. Once the team has thoroughly discussed all the ideas, time is provided for members to place the dots on the top three or four ideas they believe will best serve the needs of the school. I usually plan for this activity to occur right before a break so that members can place their dots anonymously without feeling pressured by time or individuals. Once the dots have been placed, the facilitator counts the number of dots for each area and identifies the top three or four. When the members return from break they now discuss the outcome and choose one or two areas they are ready to pursue.
- *Small Group Ranking:* Another way to ensure all members have a voice in the final decision is to divide the team into small groups of two to four members. Allow time for the members to discuss and rank in order of importance the research and possible interventions the team has analyzed. They can then place their charts on the wall. The facilitator then leads the whole group in a discussion to find commonalities among the different groups until the team reaches consensus on the top areas for implementation. At this point, the facilitator might also consider using the charts and dots activity before reaching final consensus.
- *Tabling Discussion:* When it becomes clear that consensus cannot be reached on a specific area of concern, it's time to table the discussion and move forward with the areas for which the whole

team can agree to pursue. Remind the team that if they are unable to reach consensus on the topic, it is unlikely that the faculty is ready to move forward with the plan either. Instead, the team agrees to begin with those areas for which they all agree and revisit the other areas at a later time.

Once the team has reached consensus and clearly narrowed the focus to one or two areas of concern, it's time to begin the process of learning how to implement the desired changes in their own classrooms.

Team Professional Development

Once the focus has been narrowed to one or two areas for improvement, schools are ready to begin designing their plan. At this point, the team should have a clear picture of which areas need improving and some possible solutions for improving them. In most cases, however, the team does not have the background knowledge and the educational experience of incorporating these changes in their own classrooms. Thus, it becomes important that the team engage in professional development to learn how to successfully change their practice. Engaging in professional development as a team allows the members time to identify specific practices that are more likely to be well received by the faculty while at the same time helping them to develop their own skills at incorporating the changes. As I mentioned earlier, prior to imposing professional development requirements on the faculty, team members must have experienced the same requirements. Once the plan has been presented to the faculty, team members will be able to share personal experiences related to improving student achievement. Keep in mind that if the team membership is unwilling to participate in the plan expectations, it is highly unlikely that the general faculty will participate.

> Why does the literacy team need to engage in professional development?

A small, alternative middle school in Florida noticed that students' fluency scores actually declined over the year rather than increased. They examined the literacy research and learned that disfluent students struggled with comprehension. Most of the team were comfortable with comprehension strategies but did not know how to incorporate fluency strategies in their classrooms. They decided it was important to find out more about fluency and its relationship to comprehension. They realized that as a team, they did not have the knowledge to make informed decisions about the best way to improve fluency over time. Their first goal was to engage the team in professional development to help them have a clearer understanding of fluency importance and identify specific classroom practices leading to improved student achievement.

This team understood that before they could identify an action plan, they needed to be fully informed on the best practices related to fluency. They needed time to learn about the instructional practices linked to improving fluency achievement, and they needed to have time to implement the practices in their own classrooms before deciding on a course of action.

Successful teams take time to effectively research possible solutions and consider how that solution might work in their own school community. After identifying one or two major areas of concern, teams need to take the time to engage in their own professional learning prior to deciding on a course of action.

Professional development for the team can take on many forms. Some schools decide to have the team attend carefully selected professional development provided by outside sources either by attending a convention or institute or by inviting a professional developer to the school to specifically address the leadership team. Although both of these methods can be fruitful, they may require the team to invest large sums of money and time outside of the school day, which might not be feasible.

- *Conference and Institutes:* Attending a professional development institute or conference does not allow for the team to gather collective knowledge specific to their school needs; however, members can share the information they gleaned from the conference and link it to school needs when they return. Vital to ensuring success from attending conferences is to plan for ongoing, sustained professional development once the participants return to the school. One successful school determined that its teachers needed help incorporating more small-group instruction in the classrooms. It obtained a grant allowing the school to send five people to a conference focusing on differentiated instruction. These members returned to the school and provided school-based professional development focusing on small-group instruction. The reading coach supported the plan by working individually with teachers as they learned how to incorporate small groups into their classrooms.

- *Professional Development Facilitators:* Inviting a professional developer to the team is more collaborative because the whole team can attend the same training. It also allows for more specific school-based support; but this can be quite costly. Another drawback is that some facilitators have "canned" programs which they simply repeat from school to school. If your school intends to contract with an outside facilitator, make sure the facilitator is willing to plan the professional development based on your school data and needs.

Fortunately, some districts employ staff developers who can be called upon to deliver professional development for the team. District staff developers tend to provide professional development targeted to specific school needs which allows the team more control over the content.

Finalizing the Plan

Now that the team has narrowed its focus and identified changes in instructional practices which they believe are most likely to be effective with their students, it's time to develop the literacy plan. Effective plans include four essential elements: student achievement, instructional practices, professional development, and evaluation.

> What should be included in our action plan?

As the team begins to define its plan, make sure to set achievable goals that are likely to be realized. Many schools are familiar with the term "SMART" goals. This term is widely used in business and has been making its way into educational planning for several years. Essentially SMART goals are specific, measurable, agreed upon, realistic, and time-bound. All goals within the plan should be SMART goals. It is expected that at this point in the planning stage, all goals are agreed upon by the team. If the team cannot reach consensus on the specific goals identified in the plan, that goal should be tabled for future consideration.

Student Achievement

Improving student achievement based on data analysis serves as the foundation for all decisions relating to the plan development. The ultimate goal for any literacy plan is to improve student learning. As the team begins to define its plan, the focus begins with expected student achievement outcomes. Using the SMART goal concept, consider the following:

- **Specific:** Rather than set large, abstract goals, be specific about the expectations. For example, rather than setting a goal that students will improve literacy achievement, set more specific goals such as students will improve their fluency scores or will use word parts to clarify word meaning.
- **Measurable:** When setting goals, don't forget to identify ways to measure whether or not the goals have been met. How will the team be able to measure student improvement? Sometimes this requires that the team rely on district or state tests, but other times it can be measured through teacher tests or observable behaviors. Take time to specifically identify how you will measure

student achievement for each specific goal. If you cannot measure the goal, then it is not a SMART goal.

- **Realistic:** Make sure the team sets realistic, obtainable goals. For example, if the current data suggests that 60% of students are performing below grade level on standardized reading tests, it is highly unlikely that interventions will result in 90% of all students performing at grade level after one year.
- **Time-bound:** Identify specific time limit for achieving the goal. Again, these limits should be reasonable. It is highly unlikely changes in student achievement will be noticeable after three or four months.

Notice that while these are SMART goals, they do not indicate how the school will meet them. The mistake many schools make is to stop at the student achievement goal and not make specific plans for achieving the goal.

Instructional Practice

Once the student achievement goals have been set, it's time to devise a plan for achieving the goals. All instructional practice goals should relate directly to the specific student achievement goals based on the team's analysis of research linking improved student achievement to the specific instructional practices. Additionally, it is wise to consider practices that the team members incorporated in their own classrooms rather than attempt new practices at this point. Using the SMART goals concept, consider the following:

- **Specific:** Rather than write a broad, general goal such as "teachers will implement direct, explicit comprehension instruction in all classes," identify specific practices expected of teachers. For example, if the student achievement goal is to have students use word parts to uncover word meaning, then the instructional practice goal would require teachers to teach students prefixes, suffixes, and root words relevant to their content area.
- **Measurable:** Identify how the team plans to collect data to identify whether or not teachers are teaching students word parts relevant to their content area. This doesn't have to be a standardized test. There are many ways to ascertain whether or not teachers are incorporating the instructional practices in their classrooms. For instance, the goal could be measured by having teachers turn in lesson plans focusing on word parts.
- **Reasonable:** When setting instructional practice goals it is a good idea to be realistic in the expectation that all teachers will immediately begin incorporating the instructional changes. Al-

low time for professional development as well as for teachers to become comfortable with the practice. Also recognize that some practices are not conducive to all content areas. It is okay to define the goal in very specific terms related to teacher expertise and content area.

- **Time-bound:** Basically this requirement falls within the above expectation that the goal be reasonable.

Again, notice that the goals indicate the expected changes in instructional practices, but do not indicate whether or not professional development will be provided to help teachers achieve the goals. Just as with student achievement goals, instructional practice goals are dependent on the level of support provided teachers as they learn how to implement these new strategies in their own classrooms.

Professional Development

Paramount to the literacy plan is the need to provide for ongoing professional development related to the instructional practices identified in the plan. Remember that when teachers believe that professional development has been arbitrarily assigned or that it is unrelated to their own instructional practices, they tend to dismiss the learning and focus on completing the requirements (Guskey, 2000). Therefore, effective professional development must reflect the needs of the school based on analysis of data, must provide for specific curricular and instructional changes linked to improved student learning, and must be supported throughout the school year to enable teachers to successfully implement the changes (Joyce & Showers, 2002).

Effective professional development is purposeful and relevant to classroom expectations and remains constant throughout the year. Just as with analyzing research, the leadership team needs to spend time discussing the professional development, participating in the professional development, incorporating changes in their own classrooms, and determining which changes will most benefit the school. The team must then devise a plan that allows for continuing professional development and classroom support throughout the entire year if sustained change is to actually occur. Chapter 5 discusses specific whole-school professional development in more depth.

- **Specific:** Identify specific types of professional development that teachers are expected to complete. For example: if we continue with the expectation that students will use word parts to identify word meaning, then the professional development might consist of having a district facilitator meet with individual departments to teach them how to create lesson plans focusing on prefixes, suffixes, and root words relevant to each department.

- **Measurable:** For this specific professional development, the measurement might be related to the percentage of teachers who attended the department sessions, as well as the number of departments that offered the sessions.
- **Reasonable:** Time for these sessions to occur must be included in the plan. The plan might include a directive that the sessions take place during regularly scheduled department meetings or include a before or after school session. Whatever the requirement, it must be reasonably attainable by the majority of teachers.
- **Time-bound:** Setting shorter time limits for professional development than for student achievement and instructional practices is a wise decision. We cannot reasonably expect changes in either student achievement or instructional practices if we do not provide teachers with the necessary professional development. Likewise, it is highly unlikely we will achieve our goals if the professional development is not even offered until the end of the year.

Now the team has created a plan that identifies specific goals for teachers and students, as well as a plan of action for achieving these goals. The next step is to develop a system to measure the plan's progress and success throughout the year. An effective literacy plan includes all three sets of goals: student achievement, instructional practices, and professional development.

Plan Evaluation

Designing appropriate ways to collect data to determine the effectiveness of the interventions is equally essential for all literacy plans. Some of the measurements have been defined within the SMART goals process and can be applied to the plan evaluation. Others may need to be added. All measurements must be specific in nature both in what is being measured and what is expected. For example, if our plan includes expectations that teachers will incorporate word study in classrooms, then what specific form of data will we collect to determine whether or not it is occurring and what is a reasonable expectation of success? How often will we collect this data? Who will collect it and how will it be reported to the team? All of these factors need to be considered when defining the evaluation portion of the plan.

Sample Plan

The following is a sample plan developed by a middle school. Some of the numbers and assessments have been changed for clarity.

Student Achievement

- Increase the percentage of the lowest quartile students (disaggregated by whole school and subgroups) making annual learning gains in reading from 45% to 50%.
- Increase the percentage of students making fluency gains from high risk to moderate risk on the Oral Reading Fluency assessment from 54% to 70%.

Instructional Practices

- 80% of all teachers will incorporate fluency instruction and practice weekly as it relates to their content area.
- 80% of all teachers will incorporate direct, explicit strategy instruction in classes on a daily basis.

Professional Development

- 80% of all teachers will participate in professional learning communities to identify and implement direct, explicit comprehension instruction in all classrooms using specific strategies identified by the leadership literacy team. Teams will be provided with professional books focusing on content area reading instruction to aid in their study.
- The reading coach will provide fluency professional development during regularly scheduled department meetings during the first quarter.

Evaluation

- Oral Reading Fluency assessments will be administered three times a year by reading teachers. The reading coach will collect the data and report the results to the literacy team.
- District-mandated reading assessments will be completed quarterly. Schoolwide results will be reported to the literacy team.
- Teachers will share ideas, lesson plans, and student work focusing on implementation of direct, explicit comprehension instruction in professional-learning communities. Minutes from and attendance at the meetings will be shared with administrators.
- Administrators will collect "walk-through" data focusing on observation of direct, explicit comprehension instruction and fluency instruction monthly. Frequency data will be reported to the literacy team.
- Percentages of teachers observed incorporating direct, explicit comprehension and fluency instruction will be reported to the literacy team quarterly.

Notice how each area relates to the next. Student achievement goals are linked to instructional practice goals which are linked to professional development goals. The evaluation process measures the specific goals defined in the plan. Also note that while one of the instructional practice goals is somewhat vague *(80% of all teachers will incorporate direct, explicit strategy instruction in classes on a daily basis)*, the professional development goal indicates that specific expectations will be defined at a later date *(80% of all teachers will participate in professional learning communities to identify and implement direct, explicit comprehension instruction in all classrooms using specific strategies identified by the leadership team)*. The team wrote the plan in the spring with the intention of implementing some of the strategies identified in their own professional development prior to identifying specific interventions for the whole faculty.

Conclusion

Having a complete plan that outlines the student achievement goals, sets expectations for changes in instructional practices, provides for professional development, and identifies effective ways to collect data will result in greater opportunities for success. The next step focuses on implementing the plan and determining its success.

5

Implementing the Plan

Finally, after what perhaps seems like an inordinate amount of time, we are ready to begin the process of implementing a plan. Having spent so much time developing our plan, analyzing the reasons behind our plan, and ensuring the need for our plan, we are in much better shape to achieve our goals. More importantly, at this point the team should be functioning as a whole community dedicated to the plan's success and supportive of the plan's initiatives.

The next step involves deciding on a procedure for introducing the plan in a way that encourages whole faculty participation. As with each step of the plan, careful consideration focusing on faculty needs and expectations should drive the implementation process.

> Where does the literacy plan fit within the school vision?

As mentioned in Chapter 1, it is paramount that the literacy plan be presented to the faculty as the guiding vision behind all school-based initiatives. If teachers view the plan as one of many imposed upon them, it is highly unlikely the plan will succeed. The success of the literacy leadership team (LLT) and the resulting plan is dependent upon the emphasis placed on plan implementation. Thus, the literacy plan must take precedence over all other instructional and professional development plans.

Introducing the Plan

I have attended many faculty meetings that began by focusing on what's wrong with the school or emphasizing the pressure placed on students, faculty, and administrators by outside factors. This approach rarely incites excitement for change. On the other hand, telling the faculty they are doing the best they can under trying circumstances doesn't initiate change either. The key is to create a balanced approach modeling the same concepts used to develop the plan.

Time

Finding the time to effectively present the plan to the whole faculty can be challenging. However, investing time to properly introduce the plan pays

When is the best time to introduce the plan?

off in teacher buy-in and acceptance of new initiatives. The amount of time designated for presenting the plan to the faculty serves as a reflection of the school commitment to the plan. If the plan is presented along with a string of other information at the beginning of the year, it will be viewed by some as simply an option or goal but not as a commitment.

Some schools choose to present their plan through optional preservice days preceding the opening of school. One middle school planned its presentation for the week preceding teachers returning to school and offered teachers a stipend and lunch for attending the sessions. The day was divided between whole group presentations and breakout sessions focusing on key initiatives.

Other schools have held the meetings off campus as a way of creating a less formal atmosphere. Often breakfast and/or lunch are provided. One benefit of this approach is that it keeps teachers focused on the day's activities rather than on getting back into their rooms to start preparing for students.

Although teachers often appreciate the amenities provided by the options mentioned above, if funds are limited, presenting the plan to the whole faculty on the first day back at the beginning of the year at the school site can be equally effective if the emphasis is on engaging the faculty in the implementation process. Plan presentation should serve as an invitation for teachers to become active participants in achieving the goals set forth in the plan. Take care not to limit the presentation to a list of teacher expectations and requirements. Rather, this is an opportunity to engage teachers in collegiality and discussion focusing on improving student achievement as well as an opportunity to begin providing practical professional development to help teachers immediately begin implementing changes in instruction.

No matter which setting is available for your school, it is important that you begin the year by emphasizing the rationale behind the plan and provide teachers with appropriate resources and instructional activities to begin the year. Allow time for teachers to engage in conversations and to address their concerns. Create an atmosphere that encourages *teacher input*, allows for serious discussion of the factors influencing the plan design, and promotes collegiality and commitment to ensure the plan's success.

Introduce the Team and the Vision

As the instructional leader, it is important that the principal be highly visible during this process. The principal sets the tone for the year by christening the journey and sharing the *vision* with the whole school. At this point, the principal's role is to emphasize his or her support of the plan developed by the team and create a culture of high expectations for the plan's success. The principal then turns the session over to the team and becomes an active participant. It is essential that the faculty view the principal as a willing and excited participant who is fully present during the presentation of the plan and who also participates in staff development related to the plan.

Who should introduce the plan?

The LLT's role is to introduce the plan and initiate conversations thereby setting the tone that the plan is teacher designed rather administration imposed. This should be an upbeat demonstration of the team's excitement and commitment to improving student achievement focusing on the possibilities rather than past defeats.

Begin with Data

Because student and teacher data form the foundation for the plan, begin with the data. Just as we did in the planning stages, present both student and teacher data relevant to the plan's essential elements. Focus on areas of concern, as well as areas where the school has shown success. Carefully select data that clearly summarizes the essential elements of the plan and which will help direct the conversation. Although we spent considerable time within the team analyzing and collecting data from multiple sources, care should be taken to provide the faculty with clear, concise data that allows them to see the logic behind the plan while not overwhelming them with too much data.

How do we use student data without overwhelming teachers?

Think back to the example of the K-8 arts magnet school. The school determined after lengthy analysis that its teachers would benefit from professional development focusing on small-group instruction. The team shared student achievement data and student survey data that indicated that students were not familiar with how to effectively use reading strategies. The team also presented data indicating a majority of teachers had participated in the reading strategy professional development provided throughout the previous year, as well as the teacher survey data, which suggested that teachers were teaching the strategies to their students. Finally, the team shared data indicating a majority of classroom instruction focused on lecture rather than group work. The data supported the team's conclusion that although a majority of teachers had participated in reading strategy professional development and were teaching the strategies to the students, students were not implementing the strategies and student achievement had not improved.

When determining which data is essential, choose data that supports the plan and will help teachers understand the logic behind the plan.

Support with Research

Having identified a specific need, the next step is to validate the plan by sharing research supporting the plan's initiatives. Again, depending on time and setting, this can be accomplished in many ways. One way is to create a PowerPoint presentation summarizing the significant research supporting the plan. Another is to provide articles focusing on current research to be read and discussed by small groups of teachers. This can be done by having different groups read different articles or all reading the same article. Allow time for reading, discussing, and charting responses followed by whole group discussion of the major points.

How do we emphasize the rationale behind the plan?

The K-8 magnet school's team shared research indicating that students are more likely to use strategies if they are given time to work in groups to develop independent skills. The team then unveiled its plan to engage teachers in professional development to help them learn how to increase the use of small group instruction focusing on providing students more time to use reading strategies more effectively. The team emphasized the plan's purpose was to build on the previous year's professional development plan rather than to abandon it in favor of a new approach. Teachers didn't feel they were being asked to start all over because last year's plan didn't work; rather, they were able to conclude that this year's plan was a continuation of last year's plan.

Professional Development

It is not enough to simply present a plan and hope that teachers will find a way to implement it. Teachers need time to absorb the vision and opportunities to implement the expected changes in instruction through carefully designed stages. Guskey (2000, p. 37) suggests that instructional changes should be introduced in small, incremental steps along with sustained staff development throughout the year, as a means of helping all teachers achieve the goals outlined in the vision.

What type of professional development is effective?

Time needs to be allowed to provide teachers with effective strategies to begin the implementation process. Beginning the year with professional development that teachers can immediately apply to their own classrooms stresses the expectation that changes will take place in all classrooms, while concurrently providing practical support. Effective plans include introductory professional development opportunities followed by ongoing sustained opportunities. Staff development must be designed to enable teachers to successfully implement the instructional changes required of them (Joyce

& Showers, 2002). Additionally, effective plans acknowledge differentiation among teachers and provide for differentiated professional development opportunities to meet the diverse faculty population.

Introductory Professional Development

The following are examples of various professional development activities that might be useful for the first day.

- *Department Meetings:* Once the plan has been introduced, divide the faculty into departments and provide time and space to learn how to begin to implement specific instructional practices identified by the team. This method is particularly effective if the literacy team has been actively involved in its own professional development over the past year. The team identifies one or two specific instructional practices it would like to see implemented at the beginning of the year based on the team's own professional experiences from the previous year. Team members then work with their own departments to provide professional development using materials relevant to their content areas. Sharing instructional practices that have been successful in their own classrooms with other teachers is one of the essential elements of effective staff development (Joyce & Showers, 2002).

  The advantage of this type of professional development activity is that it is specific to each content area and thus relevant to teachers. The team members serve as facilitators and coaches to demonstrate how to implement the practice and to provide guidance and coaching for teachers as they begin to apply the practice in their own classrooms. The facilitators are sharing successful practices that they have personally implemented in their own classrooms, thus validating the practice.

- *Professional Topics:* Another method for presenting professional development is to provide break-out sessions focusing on specific topics previously identified by the team. Effective staff development focusing on implementing instructional changes that have been shown to have a high probability of improving student achievement and learning is another essential element for effective staff development (Joyce & Showers, 2002). Additionally, focusing on improving student achievement encourages teachers to implement instructional changes and limits potentially distracting issues thus improving chances that the instructional changes will be implemented (Guskey, 2000). Team members identify specific research and practices that they have previously studied and that they have implemented in their own classrooms and found to be successful. In each session, teachers are provided with research linking the practice to improved student achievement and are provided with specific practices which can be easily implemented at the beginning of the year.

In this scenario, facilitators might include team members as well as outside facilitators who are experts in the field. Teachers are allowed to move from session to session either randomly or by assignment. Some schools provide several opportunities and allow teachers to choose from a menu, whereas others assign teachers to attend sessions in a specific order to ensure they all receive the same information. Some schools randomly assign teachers to groups whereas others group by department. The type and purpose of the staff development determines the grouping and assignment.

- *Whole Faculty Meeting Followed by Department Meetings:* Another way to present introductory staff development is to provide instruction for the whole faculty. This can be presented by a member of the literacy team, an instructional coach, an administrator, or an outside facilitator. Once the instruction has been provided, the faculty is then divided into departments to work on developing lesson plans specific to their content area. The goal is to have teachers work together in collaborative teams to find ways to appropriately apply the instructional practices in their own classrooms.

  For this type of professional development to be effective, members of the literacy team should have experience implementing the practice in their own classrooms and should serve as members of each department to help guide the discussion and planning. An advantage of this approach is that it allows departments to begin to form collaborative teams all working towards a common goal. It sets the tone for continued collaboration and can even lead to action research as the team continues to meet throughout the year to determine the effectiveness of the instructional changes while supporting one another.

Ultimately, the important factor is that teachers are provided introductory professional development specific to the overreaching goals of the team at the beginning of the year. Schools that postpone professional development risk losing focus on the school goals as teachers move into their rooms and begin to prepare for students. Emphasizing the specific instructional practices expected of teachers throughout the year by providing relevant professional development appropriate for the task helps reinforce classroom expectations and provides teachers with practical activities they can immediately implement in their own classrooms.

Sustained Professional Development

Providing immediate professional development designed to introduce faculty to curricular and instructional expectations is the first step in planning staff development. Sustaining professional development over the course of the year is the second step. The goal of the committee is to provide ongoing, relevant professional development that results in changes in instruction that positively impacts student achievement. Effective staff development focuses on providing information and support to enable teachers to implement expected changes in their own classrooms (Guskey, 2000). A well-designed plan incorporates several different methods of staff development that give teachers choice. The following are suggestions for providing sustained professional development over the course of the year.

- *Book Studies:* Collaborative book studies enable small groups of teachers to investigate an area of concern as a team. Participation should be voluntary. This type of professional development is especially useful for teachers who are highly motivated, who have a sincere interest in learning more about the topic, who are committed to changing their own instruction by implementing the suggested activities, and who enjoy working with others.

  The purpose is to provide the team with a text appropriate for the study, allow them time to read and discuss the text, apply related instructional practices to their own classrooms, share their experiences with each other, and give peer feedback to develop expertise. Effective teams meet at least monthly at a time convenient for the members. They share the responsibility for reading the text and leading the discussion. They set their own time lines for reading as well as for implementing instruction and sharing their experiences.

  Additionally, book-study teams should be expected to share their learning with the whole faculty at some point. This can be accomplished through department meetings, whole-faculty meetings, or by providing time for teachers to observe others implementing the instructional practices in real classrooms. Keep in mind that the goal of all professional development is to improve instruction. Sharing learning experiences between teams is one way to encourage and invite other teachers to try new practices in their own classrooms.

- *20 and Out:* Several of the reading coaches I have supported in my work with struggling schools have adopted what they term a "20 and Out" approach. This was developed by Nancy Ragland in Pinellas County, Florida, as a way to open the door to invite teachers to professional development. Nancy began the process by surveying her teachers to determine which factors might influence them to participate in professional development. She asked the teachers what they needed, and they responded they wanted practical, how-to materials; they wanted the professional development to be short and to the point; and they wanted food. Next, Nancy asked the literacy leadership team to determine the top five literacy strategies they believed were essential to meet the necessary changes in the literacy plan. Nancy then designed professional development to be presented during teachers' planning time. She promised the teachers that the professional development would begin promptly and last only 20 minutes. During that time, teachers were provided with snacks and drinks, a short PowerPoint presentation, and handouts. Nancy also arranged for door prizes for teachers who attended the "20 and Out" sessions. Attending teachers' names were placed in a drawing for coupons from local vendors.

  Nancy recognized that an isolated 20-minute presentation would not lead to the intended changes in instructional practice, so she devised a plan that asked teachers to commit to one or more follow-up activities that allowed her the opportunity to coach them through implementing the instructional practices. Teachers were given the option of signing up for a conference with Nancy, having Nancy come to their class and model the strategy, or having Nancy observe them while they implemented the strategy in the classroom. Nancy created a poster that she laminated, and she gave each teacher dots on which to write their initials. They could then place the dots under one or more of the follow-up activities listed on the poster, so Nancy could arrange a time to meet with them at a later date.

  Teachers had the option of choosing not to participate in any of the activities. However, the principal wanted to encourage teachers to not only attend the sessions but to apply the strategies to classroom instruction. As a way of encouraging teachers to participate more fully, Nancy created Literacy Professional Development Certificates that were signed by the principal and given to teachers to keep in their professional development folders. Teachers received these certificates when they completed the following:

- Attended a session
- Allowed Nancy to model the strategy in their classrooms
- Met with Nancy to plan a lesson
- Implemented the lesson in their classroom while Nancy observed, and finally,
- Conferenced with Nancy after the lesson to determine next steps.

Many literacy coaches have found this type of professional development to be especially useful for establishing their role as a supportive coach. Teachers enjoy the short sessions and the practical applications. Collaborating with the principal emphasizes the importance of attending targeted professional development while rewarding teachers who take steps to improve instruction.

♦ *Department Meetings:* Literacy teams comprised of members from all school-based departments find it effective to provide professional development during regularly scheduled department meetings. The team identifies specific strategies which they want emphasized in the departments. They then work within their individual departments to provide examples of how to implement these strategies in their own content.

This can be accomplished in many ways. The team member can serve as a facilitator to provide handouts of lesson plans or student work supporting the identified strategies. Some members create PowerPoint presentations similar to the "20 and Out" approach, whereas others invite teachers to observe their classrooms when they are using the strategy. Many departments find it especially effective to do collaborative lesson planning and then share their outcomes with each other as a form of peer coaching.

Emphasizing the literacy plan within each department serves to remind teachers of the expectations while also providing time for teachers to discuss in a positive manner how to implement the strategies effectively within their own content. Literacy team members can also report back to the literacy team any issues that arise as a result of the meetings so the team can adapt its plan to better serve the needs of individual departments.

- *Observational Classrooms:* Some schools identify teachers who are effectively implementing strategies in their own classrooms and arrange time for teachers to observe them. This can be accomplished by having teachers sign up to observe classrooms on designated days during their planning time. Some schools arrange for roving substitutes that allow teachers to observe during regular classroom instruction time.

  It is important that time be set aside prior to observations for teachers to understand what they are observing and to help them identify specific elements they should observe. These sessions should be led by a literacy team member, a literacy coach, a teacher leader who will be observed, or an informed administrator. Additionally, time needs to be set aside after the observations for teachers to debrief and discuss how they might apply this in their own classrooms. Depending on school schedules, some schools arrange for the pre and post meetings either before or after school.

- *Extended PD:* One of the most effective ways to provide sustained professional development is to use the reading coach or outside facilitators to provide ongoing professional development focusing on specific instructional practices. The purpose of this type of professional development is to emphasize specific instructional practices expected in all classrooms. Depending on the practice, this can be achieved through either whole faculty professional development or by working with individual departments.

  Prior to the professional development, information relating to the instructional practice is provided to the appropriate teachers who are then asked to volunteer to allow the coach or facilitator to model the instructional practice in their classrooms over a one or two day period. Teachers then voluntarily sign up to observe the lesson during their planning time. The coach or facilitator introduces the instructional practice to the relevant teachers in a 20- to 30-minute presentation. For some schools, this can be done before school. For schools that start early, I recommend that this session be done the day before as an after school activity. The coach or facilitator then spends the day or days going from classroom to classroom modeling the practice while other teachers observe. At the end of the day, teachers who observed the lessons meet together to debrief and discuss how they can apply this in their own classrooms.

The next step is to allow time for teachers to apply the practice to their own classrooms, collect student data and samples, and then meet together at a later date to discuss their progress. Schools that are fortunate to have literacy coaches can include time for the coach to work independently with teachers for lesson planning, modeling, and observation. Schools that do not have literacy coaches should allow for time for the teachers to meet on a regular basis to serve as peer coaches. After a period of six to eight weeks, teachers should meet again with the facilitator in a more formal atmosphere to debrief, discuss, and plan for their next steps.

I have used this method with several schools with great success. Teachers appreciate the time to apply the practice in their own classrooms and to meet with other teachers from their own school to discuss how it is or is not working.

For one middle school, I worked with another facilitator to provide professional development for the whole faculty to help teachers understand how to have students respond in writing to text. Prior to our presentation, teachers from different departments volunteered to have us model instruction in their classrooms. We found examples of text appropriate for each of the content areas in which we would be modeling. On the day of the professional development, we presented a generic overview of how to incorporate written response to text in all classrooms. We then separated to model in individual classrooms throughout the day. Teachers were allowed to visit the classrooms in which we were modeling and observe us. At the end of the day, we held a debriefing session to discuss what the teachers observed and how to implement this in their own classrooms. We returned to the school at a later date to meet with teachers to provide additional support for continuing the practice.

At another school, a high school, I worked independently with language arts teachers focusing on the same topic. I met with the participating teachers after school prior to modeling in the classrooms. The next day, I modeled in different teachers' classrooms and then we debriefed after school. Teachers then worked independently with the support of their reading coach to apply the practice in their classrooms. About six weeks later, we met after school to share student samples and discuss how to modify the instruction.

This type of professional development allows teachers to focus on a specific instructional practice over time. They are supported by working with an expert as well as by working with their peers in their own classroom environments which allows them to participate in applying the practice to their own instruction. Rather than receiving a "one-shot" approach, teachers are given sustained time to modify the practice and develop their own expertise over time.

- *School-based Professional Development Days:* Many schools plan for specific school-based professional development time predetermined by district schedules. Some only allow for one or two days throughout the year, whereas others have the benefit of weekly early release days that allow teachers time to engage in professional development during the school day. As with other forms of professional development, time needs to be allotted to present the information, to observe actual classroom instruction and/or samples of lesson plans or student work representing how the instruction is actually used in real classrooms, and to plan how to apply the instruction to their own classrooms. Additional days need to be planned for teachers to meet together to discuss how the instruction is working in their own classrooms.

  One high school divides early release time into two sections. The afternoon begins with a presentation of a specific instructional practice. This information is often presented by an administrator or the reading coach. Occasionally a teacher leader is asked to present the instruction using samples from his or her instruction. Teachers are then separated into departments to discuss the practice and plan for ways to implement it in their own content area. Some departments work collaboratively to design specific lesson plans.

  At the next meeting, selected teachers bring in samples of student work to share with the whole faculty that demonstrates how the instructional practice worked in their classrooms. The faculty then separates into departments to evaluate the practice and to discuss how to modify the instruction or increase its use.

  Depending on the practice, this process might be repeated over several months until teachers are comfortable with the practice. Once it has been established that many teachers are, in fact, implementing the practice with comfort, a new practice is introduced and the process begins again.

Without ongoing professional development, the instructional practices introduced at the beginning of the year are likely to diminish. Teachers, like most people, are creatures of habit. As the year progresses and outside stresses intervene, it is not uncommon for teaching practices to fall back on old routines. Therefore, it is imperative that literacy plans include a means of providing ongoing, sustained professional development focusing on the key instructional practices identified by the team in order to maintain change.

It is equally important to remember to provide teachers with options for acquiring the desired professional development while at the same time remaining consistent with expectations for changes in instruction. Notice that all the models provided allow time for teachers to learn about the practice so they understand how it impacts student achievement. Teachers are provided with modeling either through classroom demonstration or lesson plans and student samples to show how to implement the practice, and, most importantly, teachers are provided time to meet with other teachers to discuss how it is working and to support each other as they become skilled at applying the practice to their own teaching.

Finally, notice that teachers are not bombarded with a continuous onslaught of new and unrelated instructional practices. All instructional practices are directly linked to the instructional goals and student achievement goals predetermined by the LLT, which reinforces the desired outcomes and expectations of the whole school.

Bracing for the Storm

People naturally resist change, especially if they are happy going in the direction they have been going. We need to remember that not everyone will respond positively to the initiatives suggested. I have been involved in schools where one or two highly influential and very vocal individuals were able to completely shut down an initiative. To counter this possibility, we need to make sure we give voice to the supporters by working as a team to develop a supportive, collegial community. Just as we did within the literacy team, we must work together to build positive relationships within the whole school community and to encourage and provide support for those who are working towards improving student achievement.

> How do we counter opposition?

Roland Barth (2006, p. 13) suggests this can be accomplished by stating our expectations clearly, modeling collegiality, rewarding active participants, and protecting those who are participating. Maintaining these four elements in combination with applying effective leadership characteristics identified by Marzano, Waters, and McNulty (2005) will go a long way toward heading off resistance.

- *Stating Expectations:* It is vital that the principal take the lead in articulating and maintaining clear expectations for whole faculty participation. The principal serves as the **change agent** and prepares for challenges from those who want to maintain the status quo rather than embrace new initiatives. Inevitably, some members of the faculty will be uncomfortable with the changes and will need additional support and encouragement. However, it is the principal's role to maintain **focus** and provide clear direction to ensure the plan's success. The principal also serves as the **optimizer**, the driving force behind the plan's initiatives while maintaining a positive attitude towards a belief in its success. In order to accomplish this task, the principal must also maintain **situational awareness** and be prepared to intervene in situations that may impede the plan's success. The principal and other administrators must maintain **visibility** by regularly visiting classrooms and sharing with the whole faculty examples of successes they observe in classrooms.
- *Modeling Collegiality:* Working together as a team, the principal, other administrators, and literacy team members maintain clear **communication** between the team and the faculty. Strong lines of communication often belay misunderstandings that can quickly get out of hand when ignored. Additionally, maintaining **visibility** within the school becomes paramount to success. Team leaders work closely with faculty to provide guidance and instruction. They model collegiality not only within the team but with the whole faculty as a means of changing school **culture** focusing on the **shared vision**. Team members, including the principal and other administrators, must be visible during all professional development and be willing to share their own personal experiences as they implement new initiatives in their own classrooms.
- *Rewarding Active Participants:* Part of the plan should include ways to provide **contingent rewards** for those who are actively participating in the required professional development and instructional changes. **Affirming** and celebrating participation will often silence critics while providing positive feedback to participants at the same time. Rewarding small accomplishments as well as major accomplishments allows for more school members to be recognized and maintains an awareness of the possibility for plan's success. Few schools can offer monetary rewards, but a simple note from an administrator or department

chair thanking the teacher for participating in a professional development or sharing a successful lesson plan goes a long way toward rewarding teachers and improving collegiality.

- *Protecting Participants:* One of the sad consequences of change is that it sometimes brings out the worst in people. In an effort to diminish the success of the plan, some members of the faculty may choose to deride and belittle those who are participating and experiencing success. During this change process, it is important that principals and administrators maintain **situational awareness** and intervene when necessary. It might be necessary to have conversations with teachers who have expressed strong opposition to the plan as a means of identifying possible revisions to the plan and providing dissenters with an opportunity to provide feedback in a more positive manner. In some cases, those who oppose the plan may have suggestions for ways to modify the plan that will benefit more teachers and students. Because ignoring opposition does little to promote success, administrators are wise to begin conversations to eliminate opposition before it becomes impossible.

Teacher Validation

Along with Barth's suggestions, I would add teacher validation as an important aspect for countering resistance. Often teachers who resisted the plan find that upon implementing it, they are successful. These teachers become the strongest proponents of the plan.

I worked with a school emphasizing the use of graphic organizers in all content areas. During a whole-faculty presentation, one administrator shared the idea of graphic organizers with the faculty and then asked several teachers (whom he had previously identified) to specifically share ones they were using in their classroom. Naturally, some teachers did not see the relevance of the graphic organizers for their own content.

Several weeks later during a department meeting, one teacher shared that she didn't think graphic organizers would be particularly effective for her language arts class; however, out of compliance she included one as part of a writing exercise. To her surprise, she discovered that students began to write better papers after using the graphic organizer. The fact that one teacher who previously resisted the use of graphic organizers now came forward and shared her positive experience using them in her own classroom did more to promote the use of graphic organizers than any other professional development.

Expecting resistance and preparing for ways to counter the resistance should be a part of every team plan. Resistance does not mean the plan will fail; however, ignoring it and allowing it to fester unheeded can result in major setbacks.

Conclusion

The methods we choose to present the plan to the faculty often determine the plan's success. Careful planning will eliminate resistance and provide for a more positive reception. Allow significant time at the beginning of the year to introduce the team and the plan. Identify the key factors that led to the plan design, and provide teachers with specific professional development to immediately begin implementing the desired changes.

Follow up with ongoing, sustained professional development focused on the expectations. Recognize and support teachers who are working towards changing their instruction and have a plan for addressing the concerns of those who are resistant. Following these guidelines will provide a solid base for successful implementation.

6

Evaluating and Revising the Plan

Celebrating Successes

Assessing the Plan

Next Steps

At this point, the literacy leadership team (LLT) plan should be in place. It might seem like the perfect time to sit back and take a break, but that it is not. Now is the time to begin to evaluate the plan and support teachers as they become more involved in the plan. Team members serve as conduits for information to flow from the team to the faculty and from the faculty to the team (Fisher & Frey, 2007b). It is also important to remember that now that the plan has been unveiled, team unity becomes paramount to its success. It is easy to become bogged down with the naysayers who will undoubtedly begin to voice their opinions as they resist the changes. Planning for addressing teacher concerns and being willing to amend the plan as needed will go a long way towards preventing resistance.

Celebrating Successes

A simple way to silence the naysayers and continue to promote the plan is to celebrate successes. Keeping a positive eye on small steps teachers are taking toward achieving the goal of improving student achievement can take on many forms and go a long way toward encouraging the entire faculty. Celebrating accomplishments and providing **contingent rewards** help change the school culture by focusing on achieving a common vision. The following are some examples used by schools making progress toward their goals.

What are some ways to celebrate successes?

- *Biweekly Literacy Updates:* One principal at an urban high school sends out biweekly literacy updates that note instructional practices observed by administrators. These short e-mails included such items as noting how many teachers were observed implementing a new strategy, sharing examples of student successes as a result of a new strategy, and congratulating both students and the teachers. She sometimes highlighted specific teachers and other times mentioned general observations. Her goal was to continuously **communicate** the expectation that changes were taking place while celebrating with teachers who were trying to implement those changes in their own classrooms.

- *Slide-Show Presentations:* Several schools have created slide-show presentations using PowerPoint. The reading coach or an administrator visits teachers' classrooms while they are gone and takes pictures of student work or bulletin boards supporting effective instructional practices. They then create a PowerPoint presentation and run it on a loop to show as teachers enter the room for the monthly faculty meetings. In this way, teachers are able to observe actual classrooms engaged in effective instruction. The teachers whose classrooms are photographed are surprised to see their room highlighted, and they have the option of revealing whether or not it is their room, thus protecting their identities while celebrating their achievements at the same time.
- *Resources:* Many principals reward those who are participating in the plan by allotting **resources** through materials and/or attendance at conferences. Teachers who can demonstrate a need for resources linked to the literacy plan are given priority over those who cannot.
- *Certificates:* Some schools offer certificates for completion of professional development as a way of **affirming** teacher participation. These certificates can be given not only for attending professional development but for applying the professional development to classroom instruction either by providing samples of lesson plans and student work or by being observed by a coach or a peer teacher. These certificates are then used as part of the yearly **monitoring/evaluating** process. Teachers appreciate receiving the certificates because they serve as a concrete representation and validation of the time and energies spent working towards and achieving a goal. Some districts have adopted an online record-keeping system as a way to eliminate the paper load. However, I have often heard teachers complain they would rather receive the actual certificate for their file and to show to others. This rather elementary process is quite successful with many teachers who appreciate the recognition and thoughtfulness of the certificate.
- *Teacher Presentations:* Asking teachers to share their experiences with the whole faculty is another way to celebrate successes. This can be done for individual teachers who are experiencing success and for small groups who want to share their learning with the rest of the department. Teachers often respond more

positively to a teacher at the school who demonstrates effective classroom instruction as opposed to an outside presenter. Asking teachers from the school to provide professional development for the whole faculty or in departments not only validates the teacher's accomplishments, but it encourages other teachers to try the new practice.

- *Personal Notes:* An especially effective tool is a personal note from the principal or an administrator who notices an individual teacher who is taking risks and changing instruction. A simple note congratulating the teacher and/or thanking the teacher for the teacher's involvement goes a long way towards encouraging teachers to continue to engage in the plan.
- *Teaching Assignments:* Often teachers who demonstrate a commitment to incorporating effective changes in their own classrooms or whose students regularly show achievement gains are rewarded with preferred class schedules. For example, a teacher who takes on the responsibility for learning how to work with struggling students but who also wants to teach a particular class is given first choice for teaching that class. Take care not to overburden those teachers who have a gift for improving student achievement by limiting their class assignments, especially if they are interested in teach other classes as well.
- *End-of-the-Year Celebrations:* One principal shared that he kept track of the number of professional development hours each teacher earned throughout the year. At the end of the year, he gave each teacher a "PD Card." This card was worth "professional development dollars." Teachers earned $1.00 for each professional development hour. He collected door prizes from local businesses, and teachers then bid for the door prizes using their PD Cards. Not only was this a lot of fun for teachers, but it rewarded those who committed to professional development throughout the year and encouraged others to participate in more professional development in the coming year.

With a little imagination, the principal and the team can find many different ways to celebrate success and encourage participation. Continuously raising awareness by celebrating successes and rewarding teachers who are working towards the common goal should be an important part of the literacy leadership plan.

Assessing the Plan

Even with the most thorough preparation, putting the plan into action may reveal a need for revision. Steps for **monitoring and evaluating** the plan should be identified and implemented throughout the year as an ongoing process of the plan. The purpose for monitoring as well as the format and types of data to be collected must be clearly defined and presented to the staff prior to implementation (Taylor & Gunter, 2006, p. 117).

Effective monitoring provides us with clear indicators of what is working and what is not working which allows for **flexibility** within the plan as needed. Monitoring helps maintain the **focus** on improving student achievement by implementing identified instructional changes in all classrooms. Perhaps most importantly, ongoing monitoring helps reinforce the expectation that the whole school will work together to achieve the goals outlined in the plan. As Dufour and Eaker (1998) remind us, "what gets monitored gets done" (p. 107).

How do we determine the plan's success?

When we think about monitoring, we need to specifically identify the purpose for our monitoring and the specific data that will help us make informed decisions. Just as we did with identifying data useful for designing our plan, we need to be careful in identifying the data useful for evaluating our plan. The ultimate goal for any literacy plan is improving student achievement. However, we should expect to observe changes in curriculum and instruction prior to observing changes in student achievement. At the beginning, the bulk of our data collection will focus on changes in instruction rather than changes in student achievement. Therefore, the bulk of this section will focus on collecting data related to professional development and classroom implementation with a brief discussion of collecting student achievement data at the end.

Professional Development

Up to this point, a lot of time and energy has been spent determining the type and focus of professional development needed to improve student achievement. Now we want to determine whether or not our professional development plan is successful. Keep in mind that success is defined not only by the number of teachers who attend the professional development sessions but more importantly by the number of teachers who implement instructional changes within their classrooms.

How do I assess professional development?

- *Attendance:* Most schools have procedures in place for teachers to document their attendance at professional development in-services. This data is relatively easy to collect. However, we must remember that specific teacher data should not be presented nor discussed at the team meetings. Instead, the data should focus on the percentage of teachers who attend and the departments represented. Depending on our plan, we might examine the increase in percentages of teachers who attend or we might focus on the specific content areas and how many teachers from each content area attend the trainings. We might also want to look at the differences in numbers of teachers who attend the various modes of professional development. Later, we might use this data to compare with the percentage of teachers who are incorporating changes in their classrooms to determine which professional development opportunity is more successful.

- *Teacher Perception:* Teachers respond to professional development in a variety of ways. Some completely dismiss the time devoted to professional development by attending but paying little attention to the presenter. Others work diligently to apply what they've learned to their classrooms. Teachers, just like students, have different learning styles, which impact their response to professional development. We also need to keep in mind that teachers have different levels of knowledge related to the intended professional development. Therefore, it is wise to collect data to determine whether or not teachers believe their professional development needs are being met through the training offered. Hopefully, differences in teachers' learning styles and knowledge were considered when developing the plan. Now that the plan has been implemented, it is necessary to determine whether or not teachers are comfortable with the professional development provided. Some suggestions for monitoring teacher perceptions include:
    - *Exit Slips:* At the end of each professional development, collect exit cards from teachers to assess their understanding and to generate commitment to implementing the changes. The *3-2-1* strategy is useful for determining *3* things teachers learned, *2* things they plan on implementing in the following week or month, and *1* concern about the information. Of course, we can modify the items as needed to collect appropriate information. Simply providing the participants with index cards on which they can list ideas they found useful or topics about which they would like more information can also provide insight into the effectiveness of the professional development.

- *Charts:* Creating charts on poster board and providing participants with colored dots is another way to collect useful data. The charts might include columns that allow participants to place dots in categories. In some cases, participants might write their names on the dots if they want to be contacted at a later date. Including a space for participants to list other trainings they would like to receive is also useful for determining future modifications. Collecting this type of information provides the team with immediate feedback while allowing teachers to respond anonymously. Figure 6.1 is an example of a chart.

Figure 6.1. Suggested Chart

I will use this practice in my own classroom.	I want to know more about this practice.	I am interested in observing another teacher using this practice.	I already knew how to use this practice.	Other information I would like to receive

- *End-of-Year or Mid-Year Surveys:* Using surveys to collect data on teacher perceptions of professional development is also useful in determining effectiveness. Some schools use online surveys to collect data, whereas others use paper surveys. If using paper surveys, it is wise to distribute them during a faculty or department meeting and collect them before teachers leave. Appendix E provides a sample of an end-of-year survey that includes professional development data.

How do we determine whether or not classroom instruction is changing without overstepping our role?

- *Classroom Implementation:* We can collect instructional practice data through a variety of ways. Some require administrator observation, whereas others rely on teacher/student surveys. Again, the emphasis should be on the percentage of increase in instructional changes not on specific teacher performance.

- *Walk-Through Data:* Many schools and districts have adopted some form of administrative walk-through process. Some are generated through purchased programs; however, I have found that the most effective walk-through data is that which relates directly to the initiatives set forth in the school literacy plan. Several schools have created the walk-through document in consultation with the LLT. The document is presented to the faculty at the beginning of the year as part of the literacy plan. Professional development focuses on the practices included in the walk-through form. Administrators conduct walk-throughs on a regular basis and report frequency data or identified concerns to the literacy team. Appendix F presents a sample walk-through form created by a high school.

- *Lesson Plans and Assessments:* Another means of collecting instructional practice data is to examine lesson plans and assessments. Again, most of the time this is handled through administration. However, allowing time for teachers to work together in teams to design and implement instructional changes can prove to be an extremely effective monitoring tool as well.
  - *Collecting Lesson Plans and Assessments:* Recently, I worked with a principal who asked his teachers to turn in copies of their semester final exams. He wanted to determine whether or not the exams reflected the type of higher-order questioning that had been emphasized in whole-school faculty professional development throughout the year. He read every exam and wrote each teacher a personal note suggesting changes to consider for future exams. He also noted that a large number of teachers were still writing multiple-choice exams rather than including any type of written responses. He then invited district professional developers for the content areas to come and provide instruction on how to incorporate higher-order questioning along with short and extended responses. The departments met together with their respective professional developer to receive the instruction and were provided time to work in teams to develop lesson plans and assessments that included written responses.
  - *Team Planning:* Another way to monitor lesson plans and assessments is to have departments or teams of teachers work together to design their own lesson plans and assessments. Setting aside common planning within departments promotes changes in instruction while maintaining **focus** on the desired outcomes. Teachers are more likely to incorporate changes when they see other teachers successfully implementing the changes. Additionally, it allows for teach-

ers who are teaching the same content to create lesson plans and assessments relative to their classroom needs and reinforces the concept that the plan is sensitive to the *curriculum, instruction, and assessment* variances between content areas. Team planning promotes collegial discussion as well as improves buy-in for teachers who not only are resistant to change but who may not possess the skills necessary to incorporate the desired changes. Central to monitoring is the need to have a literacy team member serve with the teachers as they plan. The literacy team member can then report back to the literacy team concerns and issues raised during the process which can then help the team to modify the professional development as needed.

- *Teacher/Student Surveys:* Another way to collect data is to use teacher and student surveys similar to the ones used to identify areas of concerns. Asking teachers to complete surveys indicating what types of instructional practices they are incorporating in their own classrooms allows the team to consider teacher perceptions about their instruction practices. Collecting student surveys focusing on the same practices provides additional information that can be compared to the teacher surveys and walk-through data. Collecting this type of data throughout the year helps maintain **focus** while gathering teacher **input**. The data can be used to identify changes needed in professional development and support. Some schools color code their surveys so they can compare differences between departments as a means of targeting specific areas.

Student Achievement

Ultimately, the success of our goal is dependent on improving student achievement. Setting reasonable goals for improving student achievement should be a priority when developing the plan. Additionally, we want to keep in mind that overtesting students often leads to frustration and resistance from students. Most importantly, we need to make sure that we implement valid testing that will directly impact implementing effective instructional practices in all classrooms. If the assessment is not going to provide enough information to change individual classroom instruction, it is a waste of time and money. In some cases, districts already require progress monitoring data that can be used to de-

How do we monitor student achievement without overwhelming the students with testing?

termine the plan's success. There is no need to require an additional set of data if one already exists.

Let me share some examples of student achievement assessment gone wild. In an effort to meet state requirements that schools collect progress monitoring data throughout the school year, one district required all of their schools to administer a computer-based reading and math assessment. Students were required to take the two-hour assessment in both math and English classes. Data was sent directly to the district but was difficult for individual teachers to retrieve. Few teachers actually accessed the data prior to the second round of assessments. This time, students who had previously attempted to pass the assessment chose to guess the correct answer rather than read the lengthy text. Although few teachers accessed the data for either assessment, each school received notification that their students were, in fact, showing evidence of decreased achievement.

Clearly the intent of this assessment was to monitor student progress. However, no professional development linked to improving student performance on the skills measured by the assessment or on ways to modify instruction as a result of the assessment data was provided before or after the assessments. Students were frustrated at being forced to take yet another lengthy achievement test that had no direct bearing on their progress and collectively chose to "Christmas tree" the answers, knowing there were no consequences involved. Teachers neither understood the data nor were able to retrieve the data easily, thus they did not make any changes in instruction. Ultimately, the data did not meet the needs of the school or the students. A considerable amount of time and resources were spent collecting data that provided little, if any, instruction guidance.

Another example is a requirement that all students identified as performing below grade level on a state reading exam be assessed for improvements in fluency. Districts were allowed to adopt various methods of assessment. In an effort to ensure the results were reported in a timely manner, many districts decided to have their reading coaches administer the assessments and report the scores. Teachers did not administer the tests and in many cases did not understand the scores that were reported. Teachers were not provided with specific professional development to help them analyze the student results and identify specific instructional strategies that might improve student performance on the assessments. As a result, no significant instructional changes occurred. The assessment process became one of compliance rather than serving as a guide for improving instruction.

Both of these scenarios exemplify the need to incorporate appropriate assessment practices that involve teachers and students in collecting data that will have a direct impact on changing instructional practices to improve student achievement. When identifying the type of data to be collected, keep in mind that teachers need to understand how to proctor the assessment, how to score the assessment, and how to interpret the data provided by the assessment. More importantly, teachers need to understand how the data will help them adjust their instructional practices to meet the needs of their students. Simply collecting student data and making it available through some form of data base accessible by teachers is insufficient for changing instruction.

Rather than arbitrarily assign assessments for data collection, look for ways to collect student achievement data specifically related to the goals set by the LLT. Some types of assessment data to consider include:

- *Action Research:* The most effective means of collecting data is to help teachers develop action research plans. Action research can be conducted by individual teachers or as a whole faculty. The key is to use student data to identify specific areas of concern, identify specific instructional interventions linked to improving student achievement for that area of concern, apply the intervention in classrooms, and collect evidence of improved student performance. Action research is focused research rather than broad academic achievement research.

  For example, let's say a literacy team has determined that a majority of their students are having difficulty determining cause and effect in text. After providing teachers with professional development focusing on incorporating two-column notes in all classrooms, individual departments might then work as teams to create a pretest focusing on their content area text to determine how many of their students are struggling with cause and effect. They would then implement instruction focusing on teaching students how to use two-column notes. A second department-developed assessment would be given after an agreed upon time to assess student improvement in understanding cause and effect. The department would then analyze the results to determine whether or not they should continue incorporating two-column note instruction or modify the plan.

- *Progress Monitoring:* Schoolwide assessments focusing on specific literacy skills are also useful in determining the effectiveness of instructional changes. Rather than give students general achievement tests, the assessments should focus on specific skills such as fluency or the ability to identify words parts to determine word meaning. The key is to have classroom teachers administer and analyze the test results. Schools that effectively use progress monitoring data set aside time for teachers to meet in small groups to analyze and discuss the results and to plan for changes in instruction. The purpose for collecting the data focuses on determining how instruction impacts achievement.

- *High-Stakes Testing:* Clearly it is necessary to also consider the end of the year data required of most schools. All literacy plans should be developed with the goal of improving student achievement on high stakes testing. However, it is important to remember that significant changes in this type of summary data will take several years to achieve. Limiting data collection to high-stakes testing data will result in frustration and disappointment.

Next Steps

In Chapter 3, we talked about triangulating data as a means of ensuring we were not rushing to conclusions. The same must be said for triangulating data related to assessing the plan. Take care to fully evaluate a plan's effectiveness before initiating changes or abandoning it. Consider all different forms of data collection as you analyze your plan's success. Sometimes you may want to readdress an issue rather than abandon it.

Let's look at how one principal addressed the need for triangulation in order to plan for changes. I worked with a large suburban high school for two years. Toward the end of that time, the principal accepted a position at the district office. A new principal was assigned to the school. Immediately he was approached by teachers who objected to parts of the literacy plan. These teachers did not want to continue the sustained silent reading program and did not want to attend the required monthly professional development that took place during teacher planning.

Rather than immediately set new policies, the principal convened the LLT to discuss their perceptions of what was working well and what might need adjusting. Working with the team, he then developed a schoolwide survey focusing on the team's literacy plan, seeking teacher input. The survey was administered through an online survey tool. The survey results indicated a majority of teachers wanted to continue the reading program and would prefer to have professional development once a month during their planning time rather than before or after school. Had the principal responded to the teachers who approached him and not sought out information from the team and the whole faculty, the team's initiatives would have been abandoned.

Allowing sufficient time for the plan to bring about the desired results is also an important factor in determining the next steps. As mentioned earlier, realizing significant changes in student achievement takes three to five years. Focus on the instructional changes that are taking place and seek alternatives to address areas that are not moving forward. Think about ways to build on the plan's accomplishments and revise the plan as needed for initiatives that are not working.

Let's review our original planning stages. As the team works together to identify specific needs and address concerns, it narrows the vision down to two or three immediate concerns. Once these concerns are addressed, it is time for the team to reevaluate the needs and concerns that remain unsolved or that may have resulted from the plan's implementation. Effective teams are those that recognize the organic nature of improving student achievement. No single plan will solve all issues impacting student achievement.

Ultimately, the success of the plan is dependent on the team's commitment to its success. The key is to be flexible in revising the plan as needed while simultaneously setting nonnegotiable priorities for elements that are necessary to bring about the desired changes. Working together as a team to engage in ongoing collegial discussion, research, and analysis will yield effective results.

7

Sustaining the Team

Reviewing Progress

Reviewing Team Membership

Planning for Next Steps

In late spring of each year, the team needs to begin to reevaluate the plan to consider changes for the coming year. This should be a time of reflection combined with data collection, research, and planning. As the title of this book suggests, continuous improvement requires continuous planning and collaborative leadership in order to maintain progress. With the passage of time, teams will find that membership changes, students change, and goals change; thus, the plan must change, too.

Let's revisit the sports team analogy. Successful teams take time at the end of each season to reevaluate their team progress. Some players decide to retire, whereas others are traded as a way to improve overall team performance. New players are recruited and new plays are designed. The same is true for highly functioning literacy leadership teams (LLTs). The end of the year is a time for the LLT to reconsider goals, reevaluate team membership by reconsidering whether or not each member is willing to commit to another year, and examine the possibility of adding new members who might bring in new ideas or perspectives. More importantly, the end of the year is a time to reevaluate the data to determine what is working well and what needs revision.

Are we done yet?

Reviewing Progress

At this point, teams should set aside a significant amount of time to engage in review and analysis of the literacy plan. We have to remember that change often takes three or more years to become embedded within the school culture. Change must be nurtured through continuous staff development, continuous inquiry, and continuous data analysis. At each step of the process, the LLT must take time to review the plan and consider adjustments for improvement.

The most successful schools arrange a full day off-campus for this event. It takes time to review all the data and to engage in the type of collegial discussions necessary to truly examine the plan. Prior to the meeting, team members should be assigned specific data to collect for reporting to the team. It might be useful to divide the team into small groups to collect the appropriate data for each element of the plan and prepare a presentation for the evaluation meeting. Ideally, each small group would then lead the discussion revolving around the diverse elements.

Reviewing the Plan

The first step is to review the plan. Well-designed plans will guide the discussion as the team reviews each of the goals, actions, and evaluations. Questions to consider when reviewing the plan include:

- What were our goals?
- Did we implement the actions defined in the original plan?
- Did we collect the data defined in the original plan?
- What worked well within the plan?
- What might need to be reconsidered?
- Have we met our goals?
- If so, what are our next steps? If not, what might we consider as a modification?
- Do we have new goals?

Our purpose now is to look for changes in the data that can be linked to elements of the plan. Additionally, we need to evaluate data collected as part of the plan to determine which plan elements are working effectively and which might need to be either abandoned or improved. Finally, we want to collect teacher and student perception data to determine the school's response to the plan. Keep in mind that at this point, the team is not writing a new plan; rather, the team is evaluating what appears to be working at this time and what needs to be revised.

Reviewing Student Data

It might not be possible to analyze some of the high-stakes testing data at the early stages of evaluating the plan as most high-stakes testing is collected early in the spring and not available until summer. However, most schools have other student data that can be reviewed. Some data to consider include:

- What progress-monitoring data have been collected?
- Have our demographics changed or remained the same this year?
- Were there any changes in the school culture or scheduling that might have had an impact on student achievement?

- Were there any significant changes in faculty and/or administration that might have had an impact on student achievement?
- What additional areas of concern have been raised throughout the year?
- How have attendance rates, graduation rates, and referral rates changed throughout the year?

Of course, if there are other student data available that can be compared to the previous year, now is the time to begin examining it in relationship to the plan.

Reviewing Professional Development Data

By the end of the year, the team should have collected a significant amount of professional development data. When reviewing the professional development data, the team should consider not only attendance rates but should also review data indicating whether or not instructional practices changed as a result of the professional development. Depending on the results, the team may decide to repeat some professional development, abandon some professional development, or add additional professional development. For instance, if the team determines that a high percentage of teachers attended fluency trainings and were actively incorporating fluency instruction and practice in their classrooms, and if the student achievement data indicates that a majority of students are improving fluency achievement, then the decision might be to reinforce the expectation that teachers continue to implement fluency instruction in the classroom. Some professional development might be planned for new teachers if needed, but otherwise, the goal is to reinforce the instructional practice but not require additional training.

Reviewing Teacher Perception Data

Another source of data to be collected is teacher perception data. Gathering **input** from the faculty supports the concept that the plan is a collaborative effort focusing on a common goal. Most of the time, this is accomplished with teacher surveys. The survey used to identify the types of professional development preferred by teachers is also useful for collecting end of the year evaluative data (see Appendix E). The survey should reflect the specific plan elements rather than generic concepts.

Reviewing Team Goals

Part of the evaluation process should include an opportunity for the team to rethink the school vision based on the data available and the collective team experiences. This is the time to revisit the vision questions discussed at the beginning of the process (Eaker, DuFour, & Eaker, 2002):

- Why do we exist as a school?
- What kind of school do we hope to become?
- How must we behave in order to create the school we hope to become?

Reaching Consensus

Once the team has reviewed all the data and discussed all the issues raised above, it should then begin the process of setting priorities by arriving at consensus about what is working well and what needs to be adapted in the future. Several of the activities described earlier in the book are appropriate for this type of activity. Here are a few for consideration.

- Create a chart with space to list the specific actions included in last year's plan. Leave space for evidence that the action has been successful or needs to be reevaluated to be added to the chart. This can be accomplished by having the team brainstorm both the actions and the evidence. Once the team is comfortable that all the essential elements have been listed, rank the actions in order of priority for next year's focus (Figure 7.1).

Figure 7.1. Planning for Next Year

Actions Taken This Year	Evidence of Success or Failure	Rank Order of Importance for Continuing Next Year

- Have members brainstorm a list of elements they believe are working and those they believe are not working. Allow time for discussion followed by having team members place dots next to the two or three elements they believe should be kept for the coming year.

Reviewing Team Membership

The literacy team functions much like a sports team. At the end of each season, team membership changes. Some players leave and new ones arrive. Some coaches stay, whereas others move on to the next team. No matter what the outcome of the season, new hope rests on the potential for success in the coming season. So it is with our schools.

Just as we did when we first organized the team, now is the time to re-evaluate the membership. At the end of a year, it will be evident that some members have been more committed than others. Additionally, members' lives change over the course of the year. Some teachers and administrators may move on to new schools or find they are pulled in another direction. Some may simply need a break from the intense commitment or find their lives have changed in such a way as to prohibit them for making the commitment. It is even likely that at some point the principal may leave the school.

Ultimately, it falls to the principal to make the final decision as to how to adjust the team membership. The process of **affirming** membership and helping others to move on should be defined clearly and implemented impartially. Members who choose to leave the team or who are asked to leave the team should be recognized for their hard work and commitment throughout the year. The following paragraphs provide some suggestions for handling this process.

Personal Commitment

At the end of each year team members should take time to assess the level of commitment expected of members for the coming year. Depending on the school, the action plan, and the success of the previous year, levels of commitment can change each year. Set aside time for the team to brainstorm levels of commitment the team believes are essential to guarantee success in the coming year. This can be done using many of the discussion techniques discussed early in the book. For instance, members might work together in pairs or small groups to brainstorm specific levels of commitment they each believe are nonnegotiable. They can then share these ideas with the whole team while one member charts the ideas, followed by whole-group discussion. Using the dot method, members can then narrow the list down to the key elements that all agree are most important for the team's success.

The next step is to prepare a commitment letter listing the agreed upon commitments and allow members time to consider whether or not they feel comfortable signing on for the coming year. Asking members to sign a commitment letter may seem a bit intimidating, but this method reinforces the level of commitment expected of the team while still allowing members to choose not to participate.

Principal Invitation

Some schools choose to have the principal personally invite members to join the team each year. The principal meets with individual members of the team to discuss expectations for the coming year and evaluate their commitment to the team for the previous year. The benefit of this option is that it allows the members to sit down with the principal prior to making a commitment for the coming year. It also allows the principal to address concerns that may have arisen throughout the previous year and guide those members who are not committed to other opportunities in the school.

New Members

New members should be added much in the same way as the original members. It is always a good idea to bring in new members, whether they are new to the school or they are teachers who have embraced the plan over the year. Just as the plan must be revised each year, revising the membership makeup allows for new ideas and helps to eliminate any perception that the literacy team is filled with an "inner circle" not reflective of the faculty.

Planning for Next Steps

Basically, this is the point where we start all over again. If the team has successfully reviewed the plan and finalized the membership for the coming year, plans now need to be made to repeat the process of examining student data, researching best practices, and identifying professional development to achieve our goals. Part of the process will be helping to bring new members up-to-date on the team's activities the previous year. Let me also emphasize that this is a time for the team to revisit research on best practices. Here are some ideas for consideration:

- Select two to four professional books for the team to consider. The team can then discuss which of the books they would like to read further. Some teams all read the same book, whereas others divide into small groups with each group reading a different book. The idea is for the team to read something it has not read before that relates to issues discussed in the review process. The members agree to return on a specific date and report their findings.
- Identify several articles relating to relevant issues. Pass out copies of the articles and ask members to read them over the summer. For this to work well, an individual member should be assigned to lead the discussion for each article. The articles could also be assigned to individual team members to report back when the team reconvenes.
- Arrange for some or all of the team to attend conferences over the summer. Again, this should be related to the school's needs. Members who attend conferences are expected to report back to

the team ideas for consideration. In some cases, all the members attend the same conference; in other cases, members attend different conferences.

- Some teams hold informal meetings throughout the summer. Members attend when they are able as a way of keeping in touch and sharing ideas. In some cases, principals have arranged for teachers to receive stipends for attendance.

Summing Up

Working toward a goal of continuous improvement is not a task for the faint of heart. It takes time and commitment. There are no easy answers, no quick fixes, and no silver bullets. Some actions will work, whereas others will not. Success depends on the team's willingness to work collaboratively to identify common goals and invest the time, energy, and resources necessary to achieve those goals. The practices in this book are meant to serve as a guide for beginning the process. Ultimately, success depends on your school's commitment to achieving the goal.

Appendix A

Reading Survey for Students

Think about the strategies you use to make sense out of text. Read each of the following statements and place an "x" in the box that best describes how often you use this strategy: Not Usually, Sometimes, or Almost Always

	Not Usually	Some-times	Almost Always
Before reading I review the title, subtitles, pictures, and other information and make predictions about the text.			
Before reading I think about what I already know about the topic.			
Before reading I set a purpose by thinking about what I hope to learn from the text and how it relates to me.			
During reading I make predictions about what might happen next and check while I am reading to see if I was right.			
During reading I visualize the characters and events so I have a mental picture.			
During reading I ask myself questions relating to the text and look for answers to my questions as I continue reading.			
During reading I make connections from the text to my own life, my own experiences, other texts I've read, or to the world around me.			

	Not Usually	Some-times	Almost Always
During reading I highlight, circle, underline, or make note of important details.			
During reading I make notes in the margins, on Post-it notes, or in a note-book about the main ideas.			
During reading when I come across a new word, I look for context clues to figure out the meaning.			
During reading when I come across a new word, I try to break the word into parts that I know and then try to make sense out of the whole word.			
During reading when I come across a word I don't know, I skip it and move on.			
During reading I make notes of the parts I don't understand so I can re-turn to them later and figure them out.			
After reading I go back and reread the parts I didn't understand.			
After reading I discuss the text with someone else.			
After reading I check my predictions to see if they were right and make note of the outcome.			
After reading I check to see if I have answered all the questions I had while I was reading and talk to some-one about the questions that I can't answer.			

Appendix B

Literacy Instructional Practice Survey for Teachers

Think about the strategies students need to make sense out of text. Read each of the following statements and place an "x" in the box that best describes how often you model this strategy: Not Usually, Sometimes, or Almost Always.

	Not Usually	Some-times	Almost Always
Before reading I have students review the title, subtitles, pictures, and other information and make predictions about the text.			
Before reading I ask students to think about what they already know about the topic.			
Before reading I set a purpose by asking students what they hope to learn from the text and how it relates to them.			
During reading I ask students to make predictions about what might happen next.			
During reading I have students visualize the characters and events so they have a mental picture.			
During reading I have students ask questions relating to the text and look for answers to their questions as I continue reading.			

	Not Usually	Some-times	Almost Always
During reading I ask students to make connections from the text to their lives, experiences, other texts.			
During reading I show students how to highlight, circle, underline, or make note of important details.			
During reading I ask students to make notes in the margins, on Post-it notes, or in a notebook about the main ideas.			
During reading I remind students when they come across a new word to look for context clues to figure out the meaning.			
During reading I remind students when they come across a new word to break the word into known parts and then try to make sense out of the whole word.			
During reading I ask students to make notes of the parts they don't understand so they can return to them later and figure them out.			
After reading I ask students to go back and reread the parts they didn't understand.			
After reading I allow time for students to discuss the text with someone else.			
After reading I have students check their predictions to see if they were right and make note of the outcome.			
After reading I check to see if students have answered all the questions they had while they were reading and allow them time to talk to someone about the questions that they can't answer.			

Appendix C

Suggested Resources: Annotated Bibliography

Allen, J. (2007). *Inside words: Tools for teaching academic vocabulary*. Portland, ME: Stenhouse.

Allen's new book is filled with ideas and strategies for teaching vocabulary in the content area.

Allington, R. (2002). You can't learn much from books you can't read. *Educational Leadership*, 60(3), 16–19.

This article provides research and suggestions for teachers whose students are struggling comprehending their textbooks. Allington's research and expertise provide an excellent backdrop for beginning the discussion about why we need to address literacy in secondary schools.

Beers, K., Probst, R. E., & Rief, L., eds. (2007). *Adolescent literacy: Turning promise into practice.* Portsmouth, NH: Heinemann.

This book contains essays written by prominent adolescent literacy experts from across the United States. It provides both research and practical suggestions for improving adolescent literacy through student engagement, strategy instruction, and classroom culture, along with reading and writing activities. This is an excellent resource for a professional learning community.

Bernhardt, V. L. (2009). *Data, data everywhere: Bringing all the data together for continuous school improvement*. Larchmont, NY: Eye On Education.

This text is an excellent resource for schools wanting to learn how to use data to drive instruction and bring about successful changes in not only student achievement but in school culture as well.

Biancarosa, G., & Snow, C. E. (2006). *Reading next—A Vision for action and research in middle and high school literacy: A report to Carnegie Corporation of New York*. Washington, DC: Alliance for Excellent Education. Available online: https://www.all4ed.org/files/ReadingNext.pdf .

Reading Next is an excellent resource for beginning teams and also serves as a good foundation for examining characteristics of effective literacy for secondary schools. The document analyzes secondary literacy research and offers 15 Effective Elements impacting student literacy. The document can be ordered through the Alliance for Excellent Education and accessed online.

Gallagher, K. (2004). *Deeper reading: Comprehending challenging texts, 4–12.* Portland, ME: Stenhouse.

This is an excellent resource for teachers looking for practical, applicable ways to engage students in reading challenging texts. The book provides instructional strategies and practices guaranteed to engage all students.

Harmon, J. M., Wood, K. D., & Hedrick, W. B. (2006). *Instructional strategies for teaching content vocabulary: Grades 4–12.* Westerville, OH: National Middle School Association.

This book provides an overview of vocabulary instruction and theory as well as providing 42 strategies for enhancing vocabulary instruction.

Irvin, J. L., Meltzer, J., & Dukes, M. (2007). Taking action on adolescent literacy: An implementation guide for school leaders. Alexandria, VA: ASCD.

This text provides support for beginning teams who are interested in examining how to set schoolwide goals as well as specific action steps. The text provides vignettes of successful schools which have implemented sustained changes.

Ivey, G., & Fisher, D. (2006). *Creating literacy-rich schools for adolescents.* Alexandria, VA: ASCD.

Ivey and Fisher's book focuses on five Quality Indicators for Secondary Literacy: English language arts classes; content-area classes; sustained silent reading/independent reading; intervention and support for struggling readers; and leadership and schoolwide support. This text is easy to read and useful in beginning conversations about cultural and instructional changes to improve student learning.

Kane, S. (2003). *Literacy learning in the content areas.* Scottsdale, AZ: Holcomb Hathaway.

This is an excellent resource for all content-area teachers. Not only does it include practical ideas for improving literacy instruction in the content area, it is a rich resource for content-related texts that will increase student engagement and comprehension.

Keene, E. O., & Zimmerman, S. (2007). *Mosaic of thought: The power of comprehension strategy instruction.* (2nd ed.). Portsmouth, NH: Heinemann.

This new edition focuses on the complexity of strategy instruction that includes providing students with strategy instruction simultaneously with comprehension instruction. The authors argue students need comprehension instruction combined with "explicit instruction in decoding, fluency, word analysis, text structures and vocabulary (p. 28). The book is organized into chapters on comprehension monitoring, questioning, inference, affective learning, determining importance, and synthesis. This book would best serve teams who are interested in long-term professional development or perhaps as one of the selections for professional learning communities.

Langer, J. L. (2000). *Teaching middle and high school students to read and write well: Six features of effective instruction.* Albany, NY: National Research Center on English Learning and Achievement.

This document identifies six features of effective reading instruction linked to student improvement through research. It focuses on student learning and instructional practices research.

Meltzer, J., Smith, N.C., & Cook, H. (2001). *Adolescent literacy resources: Linking research and practice.* Available online: http://www.alliance.brown.edu/pubs/adlit/alr_lrp.pdf.

This site is an extensive overview of current research linked to adolescent literacy. It is organized into four key components: student motivation; research-based literacy strategies; integrating reading and writing; and ensuring support, sustainability, and focus through organizational structures and leadership capacity.

National Institute for Literacy. (2007). *What content-area teachers should know about adolescent literacy.* Washington, DC: National Institute of Child Health and Human Development. Available online: http://www.nifl.gov/nifl/publications/adolescent_literacy07.pdf

"This report summarizes some of the current literature on adolescent literacy research and practice. It is not a research synthesis or a literature review; such an effort is well beyond the scope of this document. Rather the report suggests some methods of building adolescent reading and writing skills in the classroom. To the extent possible, recommendations are evidence based." The report can be ordered online and provides a great resource for content-area discussion of literacy.

Reynolds, M. (2004). *I won't read and you can't make me: Reaching reluctant teen readers.* Portsmouth, NH: Heinemann.

This book would serve as an excellent resource for a professional learning community seeking a deeper understanding of reluctant readers.

Appendix D

Element Chart

Reading Next: Fifteen Elements of Effective Adolescent Literacy Programs

Importance: Rank each of the elements on a scale of 1–4: (4) as essential, (3) as important, (2) as less important, or (1) as not an important feature for an effective literacy program.

Presence: Rate each of the elements to indicate the degree/presence in the school: H to indicate high degree/presence, M to indicate medium degree/presence, L to indicate low degree/presence

	Element	Importance	Presence
1	Direct, explicit comprehension instruction		
2	Effective instructional principles embedded in content		
3	Motivation and self-directed learning		
4	Text-based collaborative learning		
5	Strategic tutoring		
6	Diverse texts		
7	Intensive writing		
8	A technology component		
9	Ongoing formative assessment of students		
10	Extended time for literacy		
11	Professional development		
12	Ongoing summative assessment of students & programs		
13	Teacher Team		
14	Leadership		
15	A comprehensive and coordinated literacy program		

Appendix E

Faculty Survey

Indicate the degree to which you agree or disagree with each statement:

1: disagree strongly; 2: disagree; 3: agree; and 4: strongly agree

		Strongly Disagree – Strongly Agree
1.	I feel comfortable coming to the reading coach when I have questions and/or concerns.	1 2 3 4
2.	The reading coach is available to address my concerns in a timely manner by	
	E-mail	1 2 3 4
	Office hours	1 2 3 4
	Phone calls	1 2 3 4
3.	The coach provides support for my professional growth.	1 2 3 4
4.	I trust the reading coach to maintain confidentiality.	1 2 3 4
5.	The coach takes time to learn the content I teach.	1 2 3 4
6.	The coach is willing to step out of his/her comfort zone to help me.	1 2 3 4
7.	I have worked with the coach in the following ways:	
	Coach models in my room	1 2 3 4
	Coteaching with the coach	1 2 3 4
	Lesson planning with the coach	1 2 3 4
	Conferencing with the coach	1 2 3 4
8.	I would be willing to work with the coach in the following ways	
	Coach models in my room	1 2 3 4

		Strongly Disagree – Strongly Agree
	Coteaching with the coach	1 2 3 4
	Lesson planning with the coach	1 2 3 4
	Conferencing with the coach	1 2 3 4
9.	I use the following reading strategies on a regular basis.	
	Two-column notes	1 2 3 4
	Selective highlighting	1 2 3 4
	Summary statements	1 2 3 4
10.	The type of professional development I prefer is	
	One-on-one	1 2 3 4
	By teams	1 2 3 4
	By department	1 2 3 4
	By grade level	1 2 3 4
	Before school	1 2 3 4
	After school	1 2 3 4
	During planning	1 2 3 4
	Book study cadres	1 2 3 4
11.	I would like to know more about	
	Fluency instruction	1 2 3 4
	Comprehension instruction	1 2 3 4
	Goal setting	1 2 3 4
	Vocabulary instruction	1 2 3 4
	Accessing, analyzing, and applying student data	1 2 3 4

Appendix F

Walk-Through Data-Collection Form

SLC: 9S BC CAC MS — Dept.: LA M S SS PE FA CTE WL

Focused Curriculum 4-part — *Obj. posted:* Y N — *Evident to Students:* Y N

Reading
- ☐ Words/Phrases
- ☐ Main Idea/Purpose
- ☐ Comparisons
- ☐ Reference/Research

Math
- ☐ Number Sense
- ☐ Measurement
- ☐ Geometry
- ☐ Algebraic Thinking
- ☐ Data Analysis

Science
- ☐ Physical /Chemical
- ☐ Earth/Space
- ☐ Life/Environmental
- ☐ Scientific Thinking

Writing
- ☐ Focus
- ☐ Organization
- ☐ Support
- ☐ Conventions

Student Engagement:	**High**	**Well Managed**	**Dysfunctional**		
Afr. Am. Engagement:	**High**	**Well Managed**	**Dysfunctional**		
Student Grouping:	**Whole**	**Small**	**Pairs**	**Individual**	
Level of Student Work:	**Kn**	**Co**	**Ap**	**An**	**Sy**	**Ev**

Instructional Strategies/Practices
- ☐ Coaching
- ☐ Hands-on
- ☐ Lecture
- ☐ Presentation
- ☐ Discussion
- ☐ Teacher directed Q & A
- ☐ Opportunities for practice
- ☐ Modeling
- ☐ Learning centers
- ☐ Providing instructions
- ☐ Formative assessment
- ☐ Summative assessment
- ☐ Cooperative learning
- ☐ Setting objectives/feedback
- ☐ Reinforcing effort
- ☐ Identifying similarities/differences
- ☐ Summarizing/note taking
- ☐ Nonlinguistic representations
- ☐ Generating/testing hypotheses

Instructional Materials
- ☐ Oral
- ☐ Published print
- ☐ Video
- ☐ Worksheets
- ☐ Lab/activity sheet
- ☐ Overhead/board
- ☐ Textbook
- ☐ Technology (student)
- ☐ Technology (teacher)
- ☐ Content manipulative
- ☐ Real world objects

Literacy Strategies
- ☐ Cornell Notes
- ☐ Effective Vocabulary
- ☐ Read Aloud
- ☐ Think Aloud
- ☐ Literacy Lockdown
- ☐ CRISS
- ☐ Teen Biz
- ☐ Metametrics
- ☐ Back. Knowledge
- ☐ Socratic Seminar
- ☐ …
- ☐ …
- ☐ …
- ☐ …

Classroom Environment: Safe Learning Environment: **Y** **N**

School and classroom expectations evident: **Y** **N**

PBS: **Y** **N** Elect. Dev.: **Y** **N** Positive stud./teach interaction: **Y** **N**

Evidence that the teacher is meeting diverse learning needs: **Y** **N**

Reflective Question:

Works Cited

Alliance for Excellent Education. (2008). *There's a crisis in America's high schools.* Available online: http://www.all4ed.org/about_the_crisis/students.

Barth, R. S. (2006, March). Improving relationships within the schoolhouse. *Educational Leadership,* 8–13.

Bernhardt, V. L. (2009). *Data, data everywhere.* Larchmont, NY: Eye On Education.

Biancarosa, G., & Snow, C. E. (2004). *Reading next—A vision for action and research in middle and high school literacy: A report from Carnegie Corporation of New York.* Washington, DC: Alliance for Excellent Education.

Brenner, D., Pearson, P. D., & Rief, L. (2007). Thinking through assessment. In Beers, K., Probst, R. E., & Rief, L. (eds). *Adolescent literacy: turning promise into practice.* Portsmouth: NH: Heinemann, 257–272.

Copeland, M. A. (2003). Leadership of inquiry: Building and sustaining capacity for school improvement. *Educational Evaluation and Policy Analysis, 25*(4), 375–395.

DuFour, R., & Eaker, R. (1998). *Professional learning communities at work: Best practices for enhancing student achievement.* Alexandria, VA: ASCD.

Eaker, R., DuFour, R., & DuFour, R. (2002). *Getting started: Reculturing schools to become professional learning communities.* Bloomington, IN: National Educational Service.

Fisher, D., & Frey, N. (2007). A tale of two middle schools: The role of structure and instruction. *Journal of Adolescent and Adult Literacy, 51,* 204–211.

Fisher, D., & Frey, N. (2007). Implementing a schoolwide literacy framework: Improving achievement in an urban elementary school. *The Reading Teachers, 61*(1), 32–43.

Guskey, T. R. (2000). *Evaluating professional development.* Thousand Oaks, CA: Corwin Press.

Hargreaves, A., & Fink, D. (2003). Sustaining leadership. *Phi Delta Kappan, 84*(9), 693–700.

Irvin, J. L., Meltzer, J., & Dukes, M. (2007). *Taking action on adolescent literacy: An implementation guide for school leaders.* Alexandria, VA: ASCD.

Ivey, G., & Fisher, D. (2006). *Creating literacy-rich schools for adolescents.* Alexandria, VA: ASCD.

Jacobs, V. A. (2008). Adolescent literacy: Putting the crisis in context. *Harvard Educational Review, 78*(1), 7–39.

Johnson, R. S. (2002). *Using data to close the achievement gap: How to measure equity in our schools.* Thousand Oaks, CA: Corwin Press.

Joyce, B., & Showers, B. (2002). *Student achievement through staff development.* Alexandria, VA: ASCD.

Lambert, L. (1998). *Building leadership capacity in schools.* Alexandria, VA: ASCD.

Lee, J., Grigg, W., & Donahue, P. (2007). *The Nation's Report Card: Reading 2007* (NCES 2007–496). Washington, DC: National Center for Education Statistics, Institute of Education Sciences, U.S. Department of Education. Retrieved May 31, 2008, from http://nces.ed.gov/nationsreportcard/pdf/main2007/2007496.pdf

Lyons, C. A., & Pinnell, G. S. (2001). *Systems for change in literacy education: A guide to professional development.* Portsmouth, NH: Heinemann.

Marzano, R. J. (2007). *The art and science of teaching: A comprehensive framework for effective instruction.* Alexandria, VA: ASCD.

Marzano, R. J., Waters, T., & McNulty, B. A. (2005). *School leadership that works: From research to results.* Alexandria, VA: ASCD.

Moje, E. (2008). Foregrounding the disciplines in secondary literacy teaching and learning: A call for change. *Journal of Adolescent & Adult Literacy, 52*(2), 96–107.

Moje, E., Overby, M., Tysvaer, N., & Morris, K. (2008). The complex world of adolescent literacy: Myths, motivations, and mysteries. *Harvard Educational Review, 78*(1), 107–154.

Moeller, G., & Pankake, A. (2006). *Lead with me: A principal's guide to teacher leadership.* Larchmont, NY: Eye On Education.

National Commission on Excellence in Education. (1983). *America at risk: An imperative for educational reform.* Washington, DC: Author. Retrieved May 31, 2008, from http://www.ed.gov/pubs/NatAtRisk/index.html

Spillane, J. P., Halverson, R., & Diamond, J. B. (2004). Towards a theory of leadership practice: A distributive theory. *Journal of Curriculum Studies, 36*(1), 3–34.

Taylor, R. T., & Gunter, F. A. (2006). *The K-12 literacy leadership fieldbook.* Thousand Oaks, CA: Corwin Press.

Urdan, T., & Schoenfelder, E. (2006). Classroom effects on student motivation: Goal structures, social relationships, and competence beliefs. *Journal of School Psychology, 44,* 331–349.